30 Days to No More PMS
(Premenstrual Syndrome)

A Doctors Proven Nutritional Program

THE COOK BOOK

by

Allen L. Lawrence, M.A., M.D., Ph.D.

and

Lisa Lawrence, M.S., Ph.D.

Tarzana, California

Copyright © 2004, 2014 by Allen Lawrence, M.D. & Lisa Robyn Lawrence, Ph.D.

30 Days To No More PMS, A Doctor's Proven Nutritional Program, The Cookbook

All rights reserved. No part of this book may be reproduced or transmitted in any form or by any means, electronic or mechanical, including photocopying, recording, or by any information storage or retrieval system without permission in writing from the publisher, except for the inclusion of quotations in a review. Requests for such permissions should be addressed to ALLCO Publishing.

This book is a reference work based on research by the authors.

The directions, diets, and information about managing PMS offered in this book are in no way to be considered as a substitute for consultation, management or appropriate treatment by an appropriately licensed physician.

Printed in the United States of America

ALLCO Publishing
18653 Ventura Blvd., Suite 384
Tarzana, CA 91356

Questions@30DaysNoMorePMS.com

FORWARD

No single condition has caused more havoc in women's lives than Premenstrual Syndrome (PMS). It may singularly be responsible for more real life suffering and tragedy than any other single female problem. Other than menstruation, PMS is probably responsible for more negative myths about women and femininity than any other reason. It is likely that myths about women being erratic, irresponsible, emotional, hysterical and unreliable have PMS women at their heart. Often men as they grow from childhood will hear statements such as "You know how women are!" These are derogatory and simplistic categorical statements. They can end up causing many good women much pain and suffering and even spending large portions of their entire adult life trying to overcome this indiscriminate negativity.

These myths have their origins in the misunderstood observations of women "out of control" during episodes of PMS. No one deserves more credit for defining and bringing PMS to the public's attention than Katherina Dalton M.D. in London England. Dr. Dalton, however, did not originally describe the combination which we now think of as Premenstrual Syndrome (PMS) but she did greatly define it and help it to become better recognized. In the 1950's she observed that PMS was caused by a deficiency of the female hormone Progesterone. Dr. Dalton developed the first effective treatment of PMS, using natural Progesterone vaginal suppositories. During the 1960's and 1970's PMS was still largely ignored. Dr. Dalton's persistent and frequent publications brought the word to the general population.

In the late 1970's another pioneer entered into the PMS field, Guy Abraham M.D. Dr. Abraham made the next most important breakthrough when he published article after article about PMS as a *Nutritional Deficiency-Excess Syndrome*. Abraham recognized that not only was progesterone low but that another female hormone, estrogen, was elevated. He correlated his work with work done by other researchers to prove that estrogen was elevated because of vitamin B6 and magnesium deficiencies. He suggested a number of dietary modifications as a means of treating PMS. He also suggested that a woman's diet not only affects the intensity of the PMS symptoms, but that it actually may be the cause of the PMS and PMS symptoms to begin with.

This breakthrough has allowed us to start working with women, who suffered from PMS entirely through dietary methods of treatment. After working for a while with Dr. Abraham's dietary model, we noted that it wasn't necessarily the fact that PMS women "had a bad diet" nor that they "didn't eat good foods," that was their problem, but rather they may have consumed too much of the wrong foods and too little of the right foods for their body's needs. Often while counseling PMS women we would hear comments like "but I have a good diet" or "I eat very healthy foods." We learned not to dispute this, but also not to take it for granted. Many women consumed what is often still today considered a model healthy diet - that is it would be if they did not have PMS. What we eventually recognized and found was that PMS could be created and controlled by the interrelationship of the foods which contained calcium and magnesium, Vitamin B6, refined sugar, processed foods and

30 Days To No More PMS
The Cook Book

caffeine. That is, we found that symptoms are created because of the specific combinations of food women eat.

In our clinical practice we found that while many women ate relatively healthy foods, the majority of women who suffered from PMS did not choose their foods very well, in fact they had poor diets. Their cravings for junk foods and foods which were high in sugar, fat and caffeine created a great problem for them. Many of these women came to us and said, "well I know my diet has a lot to do with it, but I didn't know what to do about it."

We also observed another group of women who believed that they in fact had very good diets. This was the largest group we saw. Their diet is one which we generally refer to as, "the Great American Diet." This "diet" consists of the most commonly eaten foods in America and these are foods with large amounts of sugar and fats buried within them. (Most often the women are unaware of the quantities of sugars and fats they actually eat on a meal to meal basis.) This "PMS creating diet" is generally made up of fast foods, canned foods, packaged foods and frozen dinners. The foods which cause PMS are those most commonly found and purchased in neighborhood markets or are eaten at their favorite restaurants. These foods are generally made from processed and refined ingredients and contain lots of refined sugar, salt, hydrogenated fats, and bleached white flour. They may be baked or microwaved and are frequently fried. These women may also have a large intake of other non-productive or non-nutritious foods such as alcohol, candy and sugary, creamy desserts, etc.

The foods in this group are also high in calcium, as they are frequently made with butter, milk, cheese, yogurt, and ice cream. Other groups of foods which often contribute to creating PMS are beverages and foods which contain caffeine such as coffee's, tea's, soda pop (with caffeine, with or without sugar) and "foods" such as chocolate which contain all three of the above caffeine, sugar and milk.

Most of us probably recognize that all of these "foods" are common parts of the American diet. Most of us eat many of these foods on a regular basis. "This is not really an abnormal diet," you say. We certainly could find most or many of these types of foods in virtually any home in America. This list includes many foods that are highly advertised on the television by famous stars who tell us if we choose to serve these foods we "are giving our families the very best." It is also likely that many of the women who recognize these foods and acknowledge eating them are also sufferers of PMS. This is no accident for as you will see it is this diet, which is the most common cause of PMS. The Great American Diet does not, however, effect women alone, for while it may cause PMS in women, it also can lead both her and her husband to coronary artery disease and diabetes. It can create their children to become hyperactive and have school and behavior problems. Their daughters will have a greater risk of also having PMS and their mother are also more likely to suffer symptoms of

30 Days To No More PMS
The Cook Book

menopause. This Great American Diet is also a major cause of headaches, constipation, stomach and intestinal problems, obesity, high blood pressure, diabetes, arthritis, general fatigue and depression. These are only a few of the effects that we are now finding associated with consuming a diet which is high in refined and processed foods.

A question that often comes up for patients and readers, "Why put so much emphasis on diet why not just treat with medications (see the sections on medical treatment)?" For us the answer is simple, while medications may work, they do not solve the problem that originally caused your PMS. We have made a conscious choice to treat women with diet rather than through a strictly medical approach. We are not against medications, on the contrary, we simply believe that dietary therapy is a more natural way of treating what we believe to be a nutritional problem. Over the past 12 years Dr. Lisa Robyn Lawrence and I have had the opportunity of treating several thousand women with PMS and we have found that better than 80 to 90% fo these women get superb results without medication using the program we outline in our book, 30 Days to No More PMS, A Doctor/s Proven Nutritional Program. Lisa, herself who has maintained herself virtually symptom free for more than 30 years with this dietary program.

We would like to take this opportunity to give special thanks to a dear friend, colleague and pioneer in the field of medical nutrition. The man who brought us into the 20th century to understand the role of nutrition and health. Mason Rose Ph.D., a Psychoanalyst, far before his time, for 40 years would not treat a patient without evaluating his or her diet. Dr. Rose believes that many medical problems could not only be eliminated - but actually prevented by proper nutrition. Our heart felt thanks goes to Dr. Rose for his help in discovering and understand the relationship between PMS and diet and much more.

Allen Lawrence, M.D., M.A.,Ph.D.
Lisa Robyn Lawrence, M.S., Ph.D.

30 Days To No More PMS
The Cook Book

(This Page Is Purposefully Left Blank For You To Use To Take Notes)

30 Days To No More PMS
The Cook Book

TABLE OF CONTENTS

Forward. iii

SECTION I - UNDERSTANDING THE ANTI-PMS DIET

Chapter 1 Understanding PMS. 1
Chapter 2 PMS, Your Diet and Your Body. 9
Chapter 3 Eliminating PMS Through The Foods You Eat. 27
Chapter 4 Supplements and How To Use Them. 47

SECTION II - RECIPES FOR AN ANTI-PMS DIET

Chapter 1 Delicious Anti-PMS Foods. 53
    Snacks. 54
    Appetizers. 56
    Soups. 60
    Salads. 64
    Dressings - Sauces - Spreads. 66
    Fish Main Dishes. 71
    Meat Main Dishes. 79
    Beef Main Dishes. 79
    Veal Main Dishes. 81
    Lamb Main Dishes. 82
    Poultry Main Dishes. 84
    Chicken Main Dishes. 84
    Turkey Main Dishes. 89
    Duck Main Dishes. 91
    Sandwiches. 92
    Grain, Beans and Vegetable Main Dishes. 94
        Grain and Bean Dishes. 94
        Vegetable Main Dishes. 103
    Herb and Spices. 108
        Herbs. 108
        Spices. 112
    Bread, Rolls and Cakes. 115
    Desserts. 118

30 Days To No More PMS
The Cook Book

    Fresh Fruits and Nuts. 121
    Beverages. 121
    Breakfast Dishes. 124

Chapter 2 Sample Menu. 127

THE APPENDICES

Appendix 1 Revised Nutritional Dietary Goals. 135
Appendix 2 Foods High In Magnesium - Desired Foods. 137
Appendix 3 Foods to Avoid - Foods High In Calcium. 141
Appendix 4 Caffeine Content Of Foods. 149
Appendix 5 Food Additives In Your Food. 153
Appendix 6 Low Fat Eating. 157
Appendix 7 Sugar. 159
Appendix 8 How To Decrease Calories and Lose Weight. 163
Appendix 9 The B Vitamins. 168
Appendix 10 Vitamin B6. 173
Appendix 11 Fiber. 175
Appendix 12 How To Eliminate Salt From Your Diet. 176
Appendix 13 Abbreviations. 179

PMS FORMS FOR PERSONAL USE

10 Most Frequent Foods You Eat Form. 181
PMS Evaluation Questionnaire (PEQ). 176
Personal Management Dairy-Daily Symptom Record. 185
One Week Sample Menu. 186
Foot Notes. 188

TABLES

Table 1	Most Common PMS Symptoms. 1
Table 2	Frequent Symptoms. 2
Table 3	More Difficult to Recognize Symptoms. 2
Table 4	Sugars Found in Foods in the Following Forms 22
Table 5	Dietary (Nutritional) Program Guidelines. 32
Table 6	Valuable Suggestions. 45

30 Days To No More PMS
The Cook Book

Table 7	Vitamin Toxicity.	48
Table 8	Fish Tips.	77
Table 9	Poaching and Steaming Fish.	78
Table 10	Cooking Grains and Beans.	98
Table 11	Cooking Grains Overnight Method.	98
Table 12	One Week Sample Menu.	**134**

30 Days To No More PMS
The Cook Book

(This Page Is Purposefully Left Blank For You To Use To Take Notes)

SECTION I

UNDERSTANDING THE

ANTI-PMS DIET

30 Days To No More PMS
The Cook Book

(This Page Is Purposefully Left Blank For You To Use To Take Notes)

CHAPTER 1

UNDERSTANDING PMS

WHAT IS PREMENSTRUAL SYNDROME (PMS)?

***Premenstrual Syndrome* (PMS),** sometimes also called ***Premenstrual Tension Syndrome* (PMTS)** or ***Premenstrual Tension* (PMT)**, consists of complex cyclic and recurrent physical, mental and emotional symptoms which occur in some women one day to two weeks prior to the onset of their menstruation, and disappear shortly after the onset of menstrual bleeding.[1]

Most Common PMS Symptoms

PMS-A ANXIETY GROUP	PMS-H HYDROUS (WATER) GROUP
Anxiety Mood Swings Irritability Nervous Tension	Weight Gain Swelling of Extremities Breast Tenderness Abdominal Bloating

PMS-C CRAVING GROUP	PMS-D DEPRESSION GROUP
Headache Increased Appetite Heart Pounding Fatigue Dizziness or Fainting	Forgetfulness Crying Confusion Insomnia

Table 1

SYMPTOMS OF PMS: FREQUENT AND DIFFICULT TO RECOGNIZE SYMPTOMS

There are over 150 symptoms attributed to PMS. For simplicity's sake we will present only the most common symptoms, divide them into three groups: Common, Less Obvious, and Difficult-to-Recognize Symptoms. PMS symptoms affect or involve virtually every organ and organ system in the body.

Dr. Guy Abraham has taken the most common PMS symptoms and defined four categories or type

30 Days To No More PMS
The Cook Book

or groups of PMS see Table 1 above. In Table we look at PMS symptoms as described by Dr. Katerina Dalton in England.

FREQUENT SYMPTOMS	
Dr. Katherina Dalton Lists the Following Symptoms as Common:	
Psychological:	Lethargy, feeling suicidal, personality changes, assault, child abuse, self injury, alcoholic addictions, anxiety, panic.
Neurological:	Migraine, epilepsy, vertigo or dizziness, fainting.
Dermatological:	Acne, boils, herpes, urticaria (hives).
Respiratory:	Asthma, rhinitis (runny nose).
Orthopedic:	Backache, joint pains, edema (swelling).
Ophthalmologic:	Sties, conjunctivitis (pink eye), glaucoma, uveitis (infection of the uvea of the eye.)
Otorhinolaryngology:	Sinusitis, sore throat, hoarseness, laryngitis, pharyngitis.
Urologic:	Cystitis (bladder infections), urethritis (urethral infection).
Gastrointestinal:	Abdominal pains, compulsive eating.
Mammology:	Breast engorgement and swelling.

Table 2

More Difficult to Recognize PMS Symptoms
This is a group of symptoms not often recognized as due to PMS:

- Uncontrollable food binges
- Inability to stop eating chocolate or sweets
- Altered tolerance to alcohol just before menstrual periods, alcoholism
- Increased or decreased libido and sexuality, nymphomania
- Difficulty sleeping, insomnia
- Taking naps or not able to get out of bed
- Decreased feeling of well-being
- Distractable and difficulty coping with life
- Need for affectionate, to give or received it
- Orderliness, even compulsiveness
- Bursts of energy and activity
- Aggression, impulse to harm to others
- Reduced performance and reduced self-esteem
- Feelings of worthlessness and diminished self-value
- Difficulty communicating with others
- Impaired judgment
- Difficulty with or poor concentration
- Easily excitable, even high strung or emotional
- Feelings of loss of control
- Avoidance of social interaction
- Restlessness
- Change in eating habits
- Hopelessness and despair
- Strong surges of fear even phobias
- Anxiety, panic attacks, agoraphobia
- Fear of death, fantasies of death or suicide
- Loneliness or wanting to be alone and avoid others
- Need for frequent or even constant reassurance
- Inability to cope with work

Table 3

30 Days To No More PMS
The Cook Book

This next group of symptoms (see Table 3, above) are often not recognized as PMS symptoms. However, they can be, if they are found to occur repeatedly during the last two weeks of the menstrual cycle and disappear shortly after the onset of the menstrual period. They would not be considered related to PMS if they occurred strictly randomly, all through the month, or unrelated to the menstrual cycle. This is a group of symptoms not often recognized as due to PMS:

DIAGNOSIS AND TIMING

The diagnosis of PMS depends on the timing of the symptoms rather than on their type or severity. Timing of PMS symptoms reflects the cyclic nature of the female hormonal system. While PMS is generally related to menstruating women, any woman who has at least one ovary, whether she has a uterus or not, can have PMS.

The three most common symptoms of PMS are: irritability, lethargy and depression. In most PMS women, the period of time from the onset of normal menstruation to just prior to ovulation is generally symptom free. PMS symptoms can begin any time after ovulation and may last until the first (or very occasionally second) day of menstruation. Symptoms are often worse in the few days or in the week prior to the onset of menstruation. Dalton uses a very simple charting system which allows women to record their symptoms and determine their exact pattern. Symptoms that occur during the period of time from shortly after the onset of menstruation to the day or so prior to ovulation are not usually attributed to PMS.

When menstrual cycles are short, symptoms may seem to occur all the time. This is usually because a cycle of twenty-one days may only have four to five days that are symptom free.

PMS Symptoms Can Vary from Woman to Woman

The Symptoms of PMS Can Vary in Type and Severity,

From Day to Day, from Month to Month, from Year to Year.

---

30 Days To No More PMS
The Cook Book

WHO GETS PMS?

The most common group of women who suffer from PMS is between the ages of 19 and 50 years old. More than 50 million women in America fall into this age group and either have PMS or are at risk of having PMS. It has been estimated that of these 50 million-plus women, 30% to 40% will experience PMS symptoms of some degree. Often they are affected by symptoms ranging in intensity from mild to severe. Most often women develop recognizable symptoms of PMS during the mid-twenties. The most common time for women to begin recognizing that they have symptoms severe enough to be a problem for them is the third decade between 25 to 35 years of age. Prior to the third decade, women have symptoms but are more likely to consider them as "normal" or "just part of life." These younger women are often willing to put up with and live with their symptoms. The majority are not aware that there is an extremely high likelihood that their symptoms will progressively worsen. Most women in the 25 to 35-age groups admit that if they had realized that their symptoms were part of a progressive pattern they would have done something about them earlier. The youngest patient we have seen with PMS was 14 years of age.

Generally, there is no racial, color or nationality predisposition. If any exists, it would appear to be entirely related to type of diet, lifestyle and nutritional patterns of the individual.

PMS AN IMBALANCE OF THE HORMONAL SYSTEM

PMS is a highly complex problem. Over the years, many scientific papers have been written about the suspected causes of PMS. At this point there is no one theory that has been universally accepted. There are groups of people who do not even think that PMS exists, while others believe that PMS may be due to a number of different causes, including deficiencies or excesses of estrogens and progesterones, prostaglandins, serotonin, dopamine, GnRH-A, or other nutritional components, etc. Some people feel it is not hormonal at all but rather really a psychiatric problem, that is, "all in one's head." Many of these groups argue among themselves, and to date, no specific single cause can be fully agreed upon.

We believe PMS can best be understood as an imbalance of the female hormones' *estrogen* and *progesterone* and as we discussed in our 30 Days To No More PMS, A Doctor's Proven Nutritional Program, we believe PMS is caused by insufficient magnesium and vitamin B6 in the woman's diet as well as too much calcium, refined and processed foods, refined sugar and caffeine in the diet. This means the defect is less of an absolute deficiency of progesterone as Dalton believed nor and absolute excess of estrogen as Abraham believed, but rather an imbalance of their relative

30 Days To No More PMS
The Cook Book

levels, the ratio of estrogen to progesterone which the woman's body needs to have to be completely symptom free. We also believe that the specific PMS symptoms that each woman suffers from are an intelligent communication from her body informing her that her estrogen to progesterone ratio is out of balance and this means that her diet is out of balance for her needs. Lastly, and possibly most important of all, her symptoms are direct clues as to how her diet is out of balance, which foods she is eating to little and which she is eating too much of. All that is necessary is that she or her physician understand how correct this and she can once again become symptom free.

We will discuss the reasons for PMS as well as the "cure"[2] for PMS. When understanding this, the reader will quickly gain an insight into what PMS is and how it can affect women who suffer from it. We have listed several groups of symptoms described as caused by PMS. Earlier, we discussed that it was through the symptoms and their patterns that PMS is recognized and evaluated. It is also through these symptoms we can determine not only the degree and intensity of PMS but what dietary deficiencies or excesses are causing her symptoms. By identifying the symptom pattern, we can even recognize the specific type of PMS and what we need to do to help her eliminate her PMS. We are aware that when symptoms occur randomly or throughout the month or with no specific pattern, it is likely (with only a few exceptions) we are not dealing with PMS that estrogen and progesterone are not involved.

Since the specific details of the causes, hormonal imbalances and the reasons why PMS occurs are adequately covered in 30 Days To No More PMS, A Doctor's Proven Nutritional Program we will not get into any of this in this book. Instead we will only look at two aspects of PMS:

1. How food promotes or causes PMS and how food can cure it.... and
2. How to create a delicious diet to eat your PMS away.

To accomplish the first part we will provide a limited review of the material covered in 30 Days To No More PMS, A Doctor's Proven Nutritional Program and talk primarily about the role of magnesium, calcium, vitamin B6, refined and processed foods, refined sugars and caffeine in Section 1 of this book. In Section 2, we will provide for you both information and recipes on how to create tasty, delicious foods and integrate this into a healthy diet that will help you to eliminate your PMS symptoms.

30 Days To No More PMS
The Cook Book

MAGNESIUM, CALCIUM AND VITAMIN B6

Magnesium, which is so important to proper estrogen metabolism, is also involved in a number of other important bodily processes, including the metabolism of sugar. When the diet is too high in calcium, the calcium competes with magnesium and can block certain metabolic processes that also promote the likelihood of PMS. The interaction between calcium and magnesium produces imbalances in still other metabolic processes which, when combined with the problems created with estrogen metabolism, further activates the complex of symptoms we think of as PMS.

A deficiency of vitamin B6 also appears to be a major factor in the creation of PMS. Vitamin B6 is essential as part of the coenzyme-enzyme reactions necessary to process estrogen into its conjugated, inactive, form. It is also facilitates the functioning of linoleic acid. Linoleic acid is necessary in the synthesis of specific prostaglandins associated with estrogen metabolism. Vitamin B6 is intrinsically connected with vitamin B12 absorption, the production of hydrochloric acid and the digestive process, as well as magnesium metabolism. Vitamin B6 is also critical to the metabolism of glycogen, the sugary substance, which provides energy for the liver and muscle tissues. Now we can immediately see how varying deficiencies of magnesium and vitamin B6, along with excesses of calcium, sugar and caffeine, can create a number of problems which add to and change the symptomatic patterns of PMS.

There are two ways an individual can become deficient in either or both vitamin B6 and magnesium. We call these processes absolute and relative deficiencies.

ABSOLUTE DEFICIENCY

An *Absolute Deficiency* occurs when an individual's diet contains less than the total amount of any one, or all, of the essential nutrients (magnesium, vitamin B6, vitamin E, vitamin D, etc.) which are needed to maintain effective metabolic processes. This can occur either when the diet you choose is devoid of these nutrients or because foods chosen lacks a sufficient amount of these nutrients. In short, these essential elements are present in inadequate amounts in the total of the foods eaten.

Absolute deficiency typically occurs in two ways:

1. Eating a diet which is made up primarily of foods devoid of adequate nutrients, such as refined and processed foods, junk foods or empty-calorie foods.

30 Days To No More PMS
The Cook Book

2. Starvation occurs when you eating too little food, such as when women are trying to lose weight and they go on a starvation diet, that is eating too few calories, salads only or significantly cutting down on protein or other select groups of foods, or when they skip meals.

RELATIVE DEFICIENCY

A *Relative Deficiency* occurs when there may be sufficient nutrients (magnesium, vitamin B6, etc.), but the diet also contains an excessive amount of other "Offender foods." These "offender foods" either inactivate, compete with or use up magnesium or vitamin B6 to create a situation which leaves the individual with insufficient nutrients to properly process estrogen and other essential functions. Foods such as simple carbohydrates (sugar, honey, alcohol, processed foods), calcium (dairy or other foods or supplements which are high in calcium) and caffeine rich foods and beverages can do this. The net result is virtually the same as if the diet had been deficient.

COMBINED ABSOLUTE AND RELATIVE DEFICIENCY SYNDROMES

We see these two states commonly in women who suffer from either an absolute and relative deficiency situation. These conditions can occur at the same time during the process of trying to lose weight, or because these women refuse to eat certain foods because they dislike them, have prior bad experiences, allergies, food fade diets, beliefs that certain types of foods (carbohydrates) are too fattening, addiction to junk foods, sugar, chocolates all of which act to kill the appetite, or with the use of excessive alcohol use, heavy smoking which can also kill the appetite. Because these women have unbalanced diets they often end up deficient in one or more types of essential nutrients PMS, diabetes, heart disease and other nutritional deficiency disease are ultimately the end result.

While we often differentiate between these two types of deficiencies for discussion's sake, in a practical sense this is of little value. The dietary program we are about to outline for you takes into consideration both deficiency types. You, on the other hand, may eventually want to evaluate your eating habits to determine which has caused your problems.

CAN PMS BE TREATED, AND IF SO, HOW?

Yes, PMS can be treated. There are two main methods or approaches of treatment: the Nutritional Approach and the Hormonal Approach, both of which we discuss in great detail in our book 30 Days To No More PMS, A Doctor's Proven Nutritional Program.

30 Days To No More PMS
The Cook Book

In introducing our nutritional approach to resolving PMS, we want to help you understand why PMS is a problem and what you need to do about it. It is essential to review the reasons why vitamin B6, magnesium, calcium and the other offenders are important to you obtaining the exact results you desire.

CAN PMS BE CURED, AND IF SO, HOW?

We have already stated that it can be cured and that the very best way to do this is through the anti-PMS diet. By careful consideration of what you eat and making sure that you chose foods that are high in magnesium and vitamin B6 and low, or better still elimination, of refined and processed foods, simple sugars and caffeine.

CHAPTER 2

PMS, YOUR DIET AND YOUR BODY

WHAT IS THE NUTRITIONAL APPROACH?

When Dr. Guy Abraham suggested that the underlying cause of PMS was a deficiency of vitamin B6 and magnesium, he recommended that treatment should be on a dietary level. The basis of his treatment program was dietary modification and vitamin-mineral supplements high in vitamin B6 and magnesium. Each woman was advised to add foods high in vitamin B6 (leafy green vegetables) and magnesium (whole grains, legumes and cereals) to her diet.

While appropriate amounts of magnesium and vitamin B6 should be supplied through the diet, it is clear that this does not happen in the PMS woman. The composition of her diet is deficient in these nutrients (through either absolute or relative deficiencies). By increasing the amounts of magnesium and vitamin B6 foods and decreasing the competing foods (high calcium foods (especially, dairy products), processed foods, sugars, simple carbohydrates, alcohol, salt, coffee, tea, soft drinks, and chocolate, the PMS woman can completely eliminate her symptoms. In fact, this does not happen without using exceptionally high dosages of vitamin-mineral supplements.

HOW TO ELIMINATE PMS SYMPTOMS

Our experience over the past twenty years has taught us that the guidelines most commonly given to PMS women (see Table 5, below), although sound, are not sufficient. To obtain complete symptomatic relief through a dietary approach, each woman must not simply change her diet. She must also become aware of the foods she eats and how they affect her. Remember, *what you ate in the past caused your PMS, and what you choose to eat in the future can eliminate it.* Simply eating a healthy diet is not necessarily enough. Many women tell us that they watch what they eat, but often they do not know enough about foods they eat to entirely protect themselves.

SUGAR AND CALCIUM

Many foods usually not considered to be sugars (for example, white flour, white rice, processed foods and even on occasion, fruits) often acts like sugars when eaten by the PMS woman. We have also noticed that many leafy green vegetables and other foods not recognized as high in calcium actually have large amounts of calcium within them. This hidden sugar and calcium may act to

30 Days To No More PMS
The Cook Book

keep women from gaining control of their PMS.

GENERAL PMS DIETARY (NUTRITIONAL) GUIDELINES

1. Eat 6 (six) small meals rather than 2 or 3 large meals each day.

2. 60-70% of daily calories should come from complex carbohydrates (grains, legumes and cereals).

3. Use fish, poultry, whole grains and legumes as your major sources of protein. Consume *no more than* 3 oz. of red meats per week.

4. Limit dairy products to *no more than* 2 (two) servings per week. (8 oz. milk or 2 oz. cheese = 1 serving)

5. Limit refined sugar to *no more than* 5 tsp. per day. Refined sugar = white sugar, honey, brown sugar, turbinado or raw sugar, molasses, sucrose, lactose, dextrose, maltose, fructose, corn syrup and sweetener.

6. Limit alcohol consumption to *no more than* 1 oz. per week if at all.

7. Do *not* over salt foods. Rather than cooking with salt add to taste afterward.

8. Use corn margarine or safflower oil margarine instead of butter.

9. *Avoid* processed foods or bleached/white flours and grains as they provide empty calories and may be metabolized as simple carbohydrates.

10. Use 1 tbsp. cold pressed safflower oil each day as a source of cis-linoleic acid. This is especially valuable for women who have problem menstrual cramping.

11. Drink *at least* 4-6 (8 oz.) glasses of water each day or more.

12. Most important *eliminate* caffeine rich foods and drinks (coffee, tea, colas and chocolates).

Two key factors are required to successfully eliminate PMS. The first is to establish a dietary intake with a relatively high ratio of magnesium-containing foods to calcium rich foods. The second is to eliminate whenever possible the foods that potentiate PMS.

30 Days To No More PMS
The Cook Book

THE TWO-TO-ONE RATIO

The foods a PMS sufferer eats must provide at least two units of magnesium (and, if possible as high as four units of magnesium) to every one unit of calcium[3]. This means consuming within each meal and snack: 2 or more units magnesium for each and every unit of calcium.
The two-to-one ratio consists of a minimum of:

$$\frac{2 \text{ units magnesium}}{1 \text{ unit calcium}}$$ In each and every meal or snack, over the entire day.

This ratio cannot be overstated, if you wish to attain complete relief of your PMS symptoms. In our nutritional program, we will show you how the two-to-one ratio can be used, easily and effortlessly. In a short period of time, you will not be able to think of any other way of eating. Once you have experienced the benefits of this diet, you will not want to go back to your old ways of eating.

Dr. Abraham's clinical work concurs with the US Department of Agriculture studies showing that more than 40% of American diets are deficient in both vitamin B6 and magnesium. This is particularly interesting in light of the fact that PMS occurs in between 40% and 60% of all American women.

In the following sections we will review both the good and not-so-good foods that eliminate or promote PMS. With a clear understanding of these foods and their effects, you will greatly improve your ability to become symptom free.

VITAMIN B6 (PYRIDOXINE)

Vitamin B6, is one of a group of some 12-15 vitamins known as the *B-Vitamins*. They are essential to humankind; we cannot live without them. Most of the B vitamins cannot be manufactured by the body. They must be obtained through external sources such as foods or supplements. Because these vitamins are water soluble (that they will completely dissolve into water and hence, blood), they cannot be stored in fat tissues like the fat-soluble vitamins A, D and E. And because of their water solubility, the B vitamins, cannot be maintained in the blood stream for any length of time. In the metabolic process they rapidly cross over into the kidney and subsequently are excreted into the urine. Vitamin B6 must be obtained on a daily basis. Its absence in the diet quickly leads to a deficiency state.

30 Days To No More PMS
The Cook Book

The B vitamins are found in many foods, but they are very sensitive to heat. Cooking, canning, prolonged exposure to sunlight, or prolonged standing, either on the market shelf or in your home, will destroy them.

The main manifestations of a "pure" vitamin B6 deficiency are the following: low blood sugar and glucose tolerance, PMT-C-like cravings, increased appetite, headaches, etc. Other less common symptoms of deficiency can include: loss of hair, water retention (especially during pregnancy), cracks around the mouth and eyes, numbness and cramps in the arms and legs, slow learning, neuritis, arthritis (with or without menopause), heart disorders involving the nerves, and muscular weakness. Note how closely many of these symptoms are to PMS symptoms.

Deficiencies of vitamin B6 have also been incriminated in fetal loss, stillbirths, increased post-delivery mortality, cystitis, anemia, colitis, prostatitis, dermatitis and many other illnesses.

We cannot over emphasize the importance of Vitamin B6 in treating PMS. Roger Williams, world renowned chemist-nutritionist believes that vitamin B6 might be the single most important vitamin of the B vitamins. Vitamin B6 acts as a diuretic, decreasing water retention. In PMS, vitamin B6 deficiency causes increased water retention. Indirectly, it can increase ACTH (adrenocorticotrophic hormone) which further increases water retention. This leads to PMT-H group: weight gain, breast tenderness, abdominal bloating, edema. Also, it may indirectly lead to the symptoms of the PMT-A group: anxiety, irritability, nervous tension, mood swings, etc.

Vitamin B6 is found in bananas, avocados, leafy green vegetables, green peppers, cabbage, carrots, peanuts, brewers yeast, wheat germ, beef liver, organ meats, halibut, sweet potatoes and whole grains. It can be reduced or used up in the body by stress, a diet high in sugar and caffeine. Fasting diets and reducing diets can deplete the body's supply. Remember that vitamin B6 is water-soluble. It must be replaced on an almost daily basis. Deficiency syndromes are difficult to treat without a diet high in vitamin B6 foods, or the use of supplements, or both. While the exact role and importance of the other B vitamins in relationship to PMS is still unknown, it is likely that they do play a role.

A deficiency of the B vitamin complex is suggested as one of the possible origins of estrogen elevation and an impaired carbohydrate metabolism associated with PMS. When the B vitamins are low or deficient, a diet high in refined and simple carbohydrates (sugar, alcohol, processed foods) can certainly lead to the PMT-C symptoms: increased appetite, craving for sweets, headaches, fatigue, fainting spells and palpitations. These symptoms appear to be exaggerated if

30 Days To No More PMS
The Cook Book

there is a concurrent dietary deficiency of magnesium. If magnesium is abundant, these symptoms are less likely to be as severe.

For those readers who are interested in the diseases and syndromes created by deficiencies of the other B vitamins we have listed them in Appendix 9.

MAGNESIUM AS AN ESSENTIAL MINERAL

Magnesium is an extremely essential mineral that accounts for about 0.05% of the body's total weight. Nearly 70% of the body's supply of magnesium is located in the bones, together with calcium and phosphorus. The other 30% is found in the soft tissues, muscles and body fluids.

Magnesium is involved in many vital metabolic processes. Most of the unbound magnesium is found inside the cells, where it activates enzymes important to the metabolism (the chemical processes during which food is used to create energy and facilitate growth) of carbohydrates, amino acids (the building blocks of proteins) and estrogen. By countering the stimulating effects of calcium, magnesium plays an important role in the way our nerves and muscles work. Magnesium is a major factor of importance in controlling the acid-alkaline balance of the body.

Magnesium, along with vitamin D, plays a vital role in the absorption and metabolism of other essential minerals: calcium, phosphorus, sodium and potassium. Calcium, phosphorus, vitamin D and magnesium must be in precise balance to facilitate the deposit of calcium into bones, as well as calcium's released from bone into the blood stream. Any alteration in their relationship will start an automatic process, shifting body stores of calcium into or out of bone tissues. The bones act as the body's storehouse for calcium. While calcium is also essential for creating and maintaining bone strength and integrity, they also require a sufficient amount of magnesium to keep calcium inside of the bones and therefore prevent osteoporosis. Magnesium ensures that calcium is both deposited into bone tissue and not allowed to leave the bone. This means that the body also requires sufficient magnesium (that is, a particular ratio of calcium to magnesium) to make sure that this is not undermined.

Another vital aspect of magnesium is its role in the utilization of the B vitamin group, vitamin C and vitamin E. Magnesium, along with vitamin B6, is required in sufficient amounts to facilitate the metabolism of simple carbohydrates (refined sugars and starches) into glucose (blood sugar). Both magnesium and vitamin B6 are also essential for the conversion of blood sugar into the energy the body needs to keep us alive, working and healthy. Without the changing of simple carbohydrates into glucose, we would die. If this process is inefficient because of lack of magnesium or vitamin B6 then all carbohydrate metabolism will become extremely inefficient and this can lead to many different kinds of medical problems, PMS being only one of the less serious problems.

In those women who are predisposed to PMS, a deficiency of magnesium may lead to episodes of low blood sugar (hypoglycemia), as well as almost all of the symptoms of the PMT-C category.

Earlier we told you that magnesium is important not only in bone growth and prevention of osteoporosis, but it is also very important for proper growth and functioning of the nervous system and muscle tissues of the body, including the heart, which is as you may remember a really large and very important muscle. Magnesium acts as a nervous system depressant by depressing the electrical conductivity of nerve tissues. This acts as a calmative. It is commonly used in the treatment of pre-eclampsia of pregnancy, a condition recognized because of its symptoms: elevated blood pressure, water retention and hyperreflexia (overstimulation of the nervous system). Preeclampsia, if inadequately treated, can progress to the point where the woman can become so irritable as to have seizures. When this happens, we call this condition Toxemia of Pregnancy. In both pre-eclampsia and toxemia, the pregnant woman becomes hyperstimulated. Intravenous magnesium is often prescribed to relax her and counteracts her hyperstimulation.

Calcium, on the other hand, is a nervous system stimulant. It is used to excite the nervous system. Both calcium and magnesium are antagonistic to each other: calcium is prescribed to treat magnesium excess and magnesium to counteract calcium overdoses.

Magnesium may also have a role in the temperature regulating mechanism of the body. It is also known as the *anti-stress mineral*, because it aids in fighting stress. It is also well known in it use for fighting depression. It also promotes healthier cardiovascular systems and helps to prevent heart attacks. When dietary magnesium is present in adequate amounts, it helps in the reduction of blood cholesterol, and it helps in preventing cholesterol from depositing in the coronary and other important arteries throughout the body, thereby reducing the occurrence of heart attacks, stroke and vascular kidney disease.

Similarly magnesium acts to prevent calcium from depositing in the tissues of the body (calcium deposits), next to or onto the bone's surface (bone spurs), and while it ensures calcium deposition into the bone. Magnesium, and not calcium, helps form the hard tooth enamel that resists decay. It can also aid in the prevention of calcium deposits in the kidneys and in the gallbladder

30 Days To No More PMS
The Cook Book

(gallstones).

Because magnesium it is alkaline, it is often used to reduce stomach acid (as an antacid), and is frequently used to aid digestion, it is commonly found as Milk of Magnesia and used to control constipation.

THE RELATIONSHIP OF MAGNESIUM TO THE FOUR CATEGORIES OF PMS

Magnesium has a number of effects in addition to its competitive involvement with calcium. A deficiency of magnesium is important in several key ways:

1. A deficiency of magnesium leads to decreased dopamine production, which results in an increase of brain nor-epinephrine and serotonin. Ultimately this can lead to irritability, anxiety, mood swings, and nervousness the symptoms of PMS-A, the Anxiety Group. Magnesium reverses this process.

2. A deficiency of magnesium can cause increased aldosterone, and therefore increased salt (Na) and water retention. The result is swelling, bloating, weight gain and breast tenderness which are all symptoms of PMS-H, The Hydrous Group. Magnesium, along with vitamin B6, working together can help to reverse this process.

3. A deficiency of magnesium is also intimately involved in decreasing the breakdown of glycogen into glucose (which is the blood sugar that feeds the brain). This provokes increased cravings for sweets and sugar consumption, and symptoms such as headache, heart pounding, fatigue, increased appetite, dizziness and fainting which are all symptoms of PMS-C, the Cravings Group. Adequate magnesium in the diet will also reverse these symptoms.

4. Lack of magnesium can interfere with estradiol (estrogen) binding at the receptor sites, and can also decrease estradiol. The result is depression, forgetfulness, crying, confusion and insomnia symptoms of PMS-D, the Depression Group. And here again magnesium will help to reverse this group of symptoms.

The end effect of these deficiencies is that a woman may develop a series of complex symptoms which we generally call PMS. They are all worsened if the diet is high in refined sugars, processed foods and caffeine.

30 Days To No More PMS
The Cook Book

CAN MAGNESIUM BE TOXIC?

Yes and No! Magnesium is generally considered to have an extremely low likelihood of toxicity. Its toxicity potential is affected by number of factors.

WHAT OTHER IMPORTANT FACTORS ARE INVOLVED IN OBTAINING ADEQUATE MAGNESIUM IN THE DIET?

In order to increase the benefits of magnesium there must be:

1. An adequate intake of vitamin D[4] as this is essential to appropriate magnesium metabolism.

2. Any calcium deficiency must be eliminated as excess calcium can predispose toward magnesium toxicity. Since a 2-magnesium-to-1-calcium intake is required to relieve PMS symptoms, magnesium intake can also be controlled by regulating the amount of calcium taken in on a daily basis.

3. Phosphorous intake[5] is also important and must be reduced during periods of high magnesium dosages. This is why we suggest lowered protein consumption in the second part of the menstrual cycle when calcium intake is decreased and magnesium is increased. Calcium-to-phosphorous should be a ratio of approximately 2 calcium to 1 phosphorous when magnesium is increased.

4. Magnesium itself has a built-in protective feature. When the consumption of magnesium is low, its absorption rate may be as high as 75%, but when magnesium intake is high, the rate of absorption may fall to as low as 25%. This feature can act as a safety device if magnesium is accidently taken in extremely large amounts, i.e., greater than 2,000 mg per day.

5. An excessive daily intake of magnesium is often controlled by either loose bowel movements or even diarrhea. As we suggested earlier, magnesium is an excellent laxative and is well known, in the form of Milk of Magnesia. One of the side effects of a high magnesium diet is that women may no longer have problems with constipation and may even have a bowel movement after every meal. If either the consistency or frequency of the bowel movements are a problem, then we recommend temporarily reducing the amount of magnesium in the diet until movements become normalized. Once comfortable, slowly increase the amount of magnesium (dietary and supplements) until a desired amount is reached, or until diarrhea

recurs. This is an important fact to remember.

As a side note, veterinarians often determine the health and diet of an animal by whether it has a bowel movement after every meal. If it does, this is a sign of health and of a good diet; if not, it is an indication of either poor health or poor diet.

6. Finally, magnesium toxicity is generally considered to be a problem if the individual ingests greater than 3,000 milligrams (generally abbreviated simply as mg) per day. Under no circumstance should our diet reach anywhere in this range. Generally, a high magnesium diet will range from 400 mg to 1,000 mg per day until symptoms are controlled and then reduced to 350 mg to 400 mg a day, depending on calcium intake. The recommended daily allowance (RDA) for magnesium is 400 mg per day.

SOURCES OF MAGNESIUM

Although magnesium appears to be widely distributed in foods, it is not very abundant in what we call, the "Great American diet" the diet most commonly eaten by the American people. That diet extremely high in calcium, fat, refined carbohydrates (simple sugars), salt and processed foods. In addition, the "Great American diet" usually includes relatively large amounts of food additives, preservatives, food dyes and colorings. You may also notice these foods have a high proportion of empty-calorie junk foods, fried foods, fats and possibly most dangerous of all for PMS women, the bleached and processed grains and flours which are devoid of meaningful nutrients. Product labeling often suggests that they are *fortified*; this generally means either that the high levels of natural nutrients have been removed and lower levels replaced, or the law requires that these products have a sufficient level of nutrients to advertise something about its nutritional value. Usually the nutrients added are in a cheap, poorly available form, they are almost always in amounts well below or just at RDA levels.

The most commonly suggested sources of magnesium are: raw unprocessed wheat germ, soybeans, figs, corn, apples, oil-rich seeds and nuts (i.e., almonds, millet, brown and wild rice). See Appendix 2 for a greatly expanded list of high magnesium foods. This list is the basis of the anti-PMS diet.

Leafy green vegetables usually thought to be high in magnesium may not be because of cooking, freezing, early picking, or prolonged periods of waiting from picking to your table. Even more problematic is the fact that in many agricultural areas, the soil no longer has sufficient magnesium or other minerals to be a good source for your needs.

Review list Appendix 3 and you will quickly see that many foods reported as high in magnesium may also be high or higher in calcium. Eating these foods could significantly alter the magnesium-to-calcium ratio and predispose to PMS. In fact, when most PMS women are questioned about the foods they most commonly eat, they will generally list foods that are much higher in calcium than magnesium. This is the basis for their PMS.

Even more important, notice for yourself how many of the foods in Appendixes 2, 3 and 7 are part of your everyday diet. If you have PMS, it is very likely you will find that you generally eat many more foods from the lists in Appendixes 3 and 7 and this is most probably why you are a PMS sufferer. Eventually, when you no longer have PMS symptoms, you will find that your diet will consist of more of the foods found listed in Appendix 2.

In the next section, we will take a look at the foods that cause PMS and worsen it these foods are the ones we call the offenders.

THE OFFENDERS: CALCIUM - CAFFEINE - FOOD ADDITIVES - SALT

It should be clear now that vitamin B6 and magnesium have extremely beneficial effects on both estrogen metabolism and carbohydrate metabolism. You will recall that we discussed absolute and relative deficiency patterns and how these can lead to PMS. In discussing relative deficiency patterns, we suggest that the major problem is not necessarily insufficient or low amounts of magnesium and/or vitamin B6 in the diet. Instead, it is too much of the competing or offending foods. We identified these foods as high in one or a combination of "offender" ingredients such as, calcium, sugar, caffeine, food additives, colorings, dyes or preservatives.

Now it is time to look at each of these entities separately to understand what they are and how they affect PMS.

CALCIUM

Calcium is the most abundant mineral in the human body. About 99% is deposited within the bones and teeth. The remaining 1% can be found in the soft tissues, cells and fluids of the body. If it is to function properly, calcium must be accompanied by magnesium, phosphorus, and Vitamins A, C, and D. Calcium and magnesium are partners in maintaining cardiovascular health.

30 Days To No More PMS
The Cook Book

Calcium is important in the blood clotting process, and in muscle growth, muscle contraction, nerve function and impulse transmission. It also plays a role in iron metabolism, while helping to activate several enzymes and regulate passage of nutrients in and out of the cell wall. The most reported sources of calcium are dairy and milk products. However, it is commonly found in many vegetables and other foods (See Appendix 3).

Calcium absorption is generally very inefficient. Usually, about 20%-30% of the calcium consumed is absorbed. Milk, once thought to be an excellent source of calcium, is now known to be a poor source of available calcium because of its high levels of potassium and phosphorus.

Calcium is ten times more abundant in dairy products than is magnesium. Calcium is probably 15-20 times more common in foods that make up the usual PMS woman's diet. According to Dr. Guy Abraham, the PMS woman should ingest at least two units of magnesium to every one unit of calcium, if she wishes to prevent PMS symptoms. It is easy to see in women with severe PMS that their only way to reverse or prevent their symptoms may be to reduce dietary calcium (working on reducing refined and processed foods, simple sugars and caffeine should always come first) and increase dietary magnesium. This does not imply a *low* calcium diet. We would rather refer to it as a better balance between calcium and magnesium. Many women worry about that, but when they lower their excess calcium and increase their overall magnesium intake (as we are suggesting that you do) you will actually have a reduced risk of suffering from osteoporosis.

When your diet is high in calcium and adequate amounts of magnesium are not available to force calcium into your bones calcium will simply circulate around in your blood stream until it is either used up or excreted. When you eat a large meal, one which is high in calcium, your blood levels of calcium will go up. As the calcium is used or excreted the calcium levels of your blood will fall, if eat every few hours the calcium in your blood will stay stable. If however, you skip a meal, or do not eat regularly, the levels of calcium in your blood will begin to fall, if your body is not getting a new supply of calcium your body will begin to take calcium out of your bones to help raise your blood levels up to your previous high. Since there is little or no magnesium to force this calcium back into the bones or keep it from leaving your bones, if this happens long enough and over many years, you will ultimately develop osteoporosis.

If you eat high levels of magnesium (greater than 2 magnesium for each unit of calcium) the calcium level in the blood will never reach a high levels as calcium will be regularly forced into your bones and osteoporosis cannot occur.

30 Days To No More PMS
The Cook Book

The average person, man, woman and child, has a diet many times higher in calcium than is actually necessary. Since the American diet (and that in most other western nations, as well) are low in magnesium, the end result is that the ingested calcium cannot get **into** the bones it will therefore end up being deposited **onto** the bones, causing degenerative or osteoarthritis. When dietary calcium is lowered (not eliminated nor even a low calcium diet but a normal calcium diet, with somewhere around 800 mg to 1,200 mg per day) and magnesium is normalized not only is PMS improved or eliminated, but osteoarthritis and hardening of the arteries are prevented. When calcium levels stay at reasonable levels and calcium is forced into the bones because of adequate magnesium, the risk of osteoporosis is also reduced. Everyone wins!

CAFFEINE

In recent years caffeine has come under fire for its many negative effects. It has been viewed as a cause of fibrocystic disease of the breasts, and incriminated in its relationship to PMS, its potential as a causative factor in cancer, heart arrhythmias and even birth defects. In addition to all of this, doctors and consumers alike have become increasingly aware of how caffeine affects the nervous system by stimulating it. These stimulatory effects were once the main reason for adding caffeine to many products from aspirin to colas. It is now recognized as not only unnecessary but even detrimental. Appendix 4 lists the caffeine content of many common foods.

Caffeine stimulates the stress response and requires B vitamins for its breakdown and metabolism. Diets high in caffeine increase the relative deficiencies of magnesium and B vitamins. Because of these functions it increases the likelihood of low blood sugar (hypoglycemia). Caffeine also kills the appetite, which leads to further imbalances and nutritional deficiencies.

FOOD ADDITIVES

The exact manner in which food additives affect PMS is still unknown. There are more than 2,000 known food additives which range from colorings, dyes, preservatives, enhancers, tenderizers, stabilizers, emulsifiers, deodorizers, antibacterial agents and insecticides. Many of these chemicals re not inert but rather have one or more meaningful actions in the body. Through the years, many have been found to be harmful. They are associated with allergic reaction and as well as toxic reactions. Some have even been incriminated in causing cancer and contributing to other major health risks. Some people believe that some of these chemicals may potentiate or worsen PMS symptoms. This is thought to be affected by further exaggerating the deficiency of the B-complex vitamins or magnesium, or both. Many of these substances act as toxic chemicals which stress the

30 Days To No More PMS
The Cook Book

body and therefore require either the B-Vitamin complex and/or magnesium to inactivate them. (See Appendix 5 for a list of the most common additives, preservatives, food dyes and colorings.)

SALT - SODIUM

Whenever swelling of extremities or headache occur as symptoms, most medical professionals are trained to think *salt*. Salt better known by its chemical designation, *sodium chloride*, is a very basic compound essential for life. The exact relationship of salt and PMS symptoms is not yet known. We do, however, recognize that there is a relationship between PMS and salt intake, but that relationship is small and often quite insignificant. The edema and swelling most women are worried about is not entirely related to salt intake. Instead, it is specifically involved with the combination of increased sugars, simple carbohydrates, calcium and the hormonal changes of PMS. A high salt intake may slightly worsen this reaction, but our experience demonstrates that it does not necessarily cause it.

Increased consumption of refined sugars, when coupled with an excess of calcium along with deficiencies of magnesium and vitamin B6, lead to increased sodium and water retention. This is the main problem in the PMT-H group described by Dr. Abraham. The majority of women who suffer from swelling of their extremities, headaches, weight gain and bloating are best served by reducing excessive sugars and calcium in their diet.

We do recognize that a diet high in salt is likely, however, to worsen the problem. In such cases, excessive salt should be avoided. Normal amounts of salt *should not*, cause a problem and can be safely used. See Appendix 12, for a list of salt in commonly used foods. We strongly recommend that women learn to cook without salt and then later add to taste.

SIMPLE AND REFINED CARBOHYDRATES — "WHITE" OR "TABLE" SUGARS

Sugars are part of the food group known as *carbohydrates*. Carbohydrates are made up of three types substances which occur in foods and living tissues: sugars, starches, and cellulose. In human beings they have two major purposes 1) to provide energy, and 2) particularly the cellulose that usually surrounds the sugars and starch, to add bulk to the diet, to cleanse the bowel and to prevent constipation. We will discuss sugars and starches only in this section. Cellulose, or fiber as it is often called, is not specifically relevant to PMS but rather only to a balanced and healthy diet. Fiber is covered in Appendix 11. In nature, that is in whole foods, these sugars and starches are made up of complex molecules. They are found most abundantly in raw fruits and vegetables. Over

30 Days To No More PMS
The Cook Book

the span of human kinds existence these foods have been used to nourish and support humans. Their digestive systems are geared to breaking down these complex molecules. In fact, one might say that our digestive system is dependant on these foods, in their most natural form, to provide optimal nutrition and support to maintain human life and well-being.

Today there are two groups, sugar and starches, we are generally interested in, those which are natural coming from whole foods and those that are refined or processed, this last group includes white table sugars, honey, white flour, white bread, corn starch, modified food starch, white polished rice, candy (especially chocolate), cookies, regular non-diet soda pops, alcohol, jams, jellies, syrups (this means even syrups in medicines), and all of the foods that are made up of or made with these substances. (For a more complete list of simple carbohydrates in commonly used foods, see Appendix 7.) When breads and products made with flour are also made with white bleached flour, even when the label says they contain *whole wheat flour,* often act more like simple carbohydrates than complex carbohydrates because of the white bleached flour in them. When you look at a label and you see ingredients such as: sugar, honey, corn sweetener, corn syrup, corn starch, modified food starch, and molasses, these are all simple carbohydrates, i.e., *simple sugars.* Therefore, when we refer to *sugar,* we are referring to **ALL** foods that act like a 'sugar' when the body metabolizes them whether we think of them as a sugar or not. We may, therefore, include some foods which you might not have previously considered to be a *sugar*. (See Table 4, below.)

SUGAR FOUND IN FOODS IN THE FOLLOWING FORMS

White table sugar, turbinado sugar, brown sugar, honey, molasses, corn sweetener, corn syrup, any foods which may end in -ose: fructose, dextrose, maltose, dextro-maltose or malto-dextrose, barley sweetener, corn starch and modified food starches, alcohol, white flour, bleached flour, white rice, rice flour, rice vinegar and rice sweetener and processed mashed potatoes.

Table 4

This is important because our body is not designed to easily utilize refined sugars and starches. They are much more difficult and take much more energy to metabolize than the natural complex sugars and starches. Because our body is not able to easily use refined and processed sugars and starches it not only has to work harder, but it also depletes our body of nutrients essential to maintaining our overall health and nutritional balance, hence eating a diet which is predominately

30 Days To No More PMS
The Cook Book

high in processed and refined sugars and starches such as the Great American Diet, increases our chances of a host of medical problems including PMS, but also cardiovascular disease, diabetes, hypertension to name only a few.

This is often a difficult concept to accept. We usually do not think of foods as causing illness, but rather of helping us prevent or treat them. This is no longer true.

Most people generally think of only certain types of foods, for example, white table sugar, as a sugar. To assure the best possible results in treating PMS, you will need to think differently. If we are going to eliminate those foods that promote PMS, we must know what they are and why they are a problem. We must now consider that all the foods listed above, as well as, any foods which may end in *-ose*: such as maltose, sucrose, dextrose and fructose, if they are in a box, can, package, should be treated as a simple sugar, see Appendix 7 for a list of some such foods. Often, so-called "*natural sugars*," such as fructose, may be *added* to foods. Once fructose is removed from its natural source, it automatically becomes a processed food and is more or less artificial, a simple carbohydrate. To say it straight forward, these "natural" sugars, when not in the original live fruit or vegetable, are best considered to be "simple sugars" and they will promote PMS.

COMPLEX CARBOHYDRATES

So far, we have only discussed simple carbohydrates or simple sugars. There is, however, a second group of carbohydrates, *complex carbohydrates*. Complex carbohydrates do not act like simple sugars. These carbohydrates are processed by your body in an entirely different way. While PMS women do not want too much refined or simple sugars in their diet, they definitely want complex carbohydrates in their diet, for they actually prevent many of the problems of PMS. The complex carbohydrate group is made up of fresh vegetables, whole grains, whole potatoes, fresh corn and fresh fruits. These foods are also generally high in cellulose and their starches provide a slower burning energy than simple sugars. Your body can use complex carbohydrate more economically then it can use simple sugars and starches. Besides, since fresh vegetables, whole grains, whole potatoes, fresh corn and fresh fruits are whole and complete foods, they usually also come with their full compliment of vitamins, minerals and other essential nutrients and enzymes which your body will need to metabolize them. In fact, in most cases they also bring an excess of essential nutrients into your body to replenish your depleted stores and then add to your stores. These are the best foods to keep you health and vibrant.

30 Days To No More PMS
The Cook Book

PROCESSED AND REFINED FOODS

As a general rule, any food in a box, a can, a package, wrapped in cellophane, or frozen (with the exception of flash-frozen vegetables), mixed with any artificial ingredients, cooked or recombined, or any foods that require you to add something, including water, are in all probability a *processed* or *refined* food. These foods should be strictly avoided during the second part of the cycle by all women with mild PMS, and all month by women with moderate or severe PMS. Processed and refined foods tend to act like simple carbohydrates. Their treatment during their processing and refining tends to change complex carbohydrates into simple carbohydrates. This makes them especially dangerous to the PMS woman.

Symptoms such as cravings for sweets and hypoglycemia (low blood sugar) with fainting, sweating, dizziness, palpitations, or headaches, should suggest an excessive intake of refined sugars. This situation occurs, if you remember from our prior discussion, because the brain can only use glucose as its source of energy. Glucose comes from the breakdown of glycogen by the liver. Refined sugars require a complex process to produce glycogen. This series of processes requires magnesium and vitamin B6 in addition to many other nutrients. Natural sugars and complex carbohydrates are also changed into glycogen, but this process is much different and far easier on the body.

Hopefully, it is now clear why the need for vitamin B6 and magnesium becomes greater as the diet increases in refined and processed foods. The impairment of the glycogen metabolism creates a signal telling your body that more energy is needed. This is transformed by your body into a craving for more sweets. If response to these cravings is consumption of more refined sugars, then more insulin is released. Circulating sugars are immediately burned up and the process repeats itself. This is part of the mechanism of PMS. It creates a vicious and uncomfortable cycle.

CHOCOLATE

"Why is chocolate such a problem for the PMS woman?" This is a question that seems to fascinate just about everyone. We previously discussed in 30 Days To No More PMS, A Doctor's Proven Nutritional Program, addiction to chocolate is almost diagnostic of PMS. The PMS woman may often be recognized by her need to have and eat chocolate. Why chocolate? Chocolate is a triple-threat food. It not only has large amounts of sugar, calcium (milk chocolate) and caffeine, but it is also very high in magnesium.

30 Days To No More PMS
The Cook Book

It has been theorized that the body craves chocolate for its magnesium and its sugar but the sugar, calcium and caffeine ultimately overwhelm the benefits of the magnesium and sabotage the woman. We definitely agree that many PMS women appear to crave chocolate. Some of these women may worry that they will have to *give up their chocolate*. Interestingly enough, when the diet is appropriately corrected, most women will lose their excessive urges for chocolate quite rapidly and after a while they often seem be able to no longer even care much about chocolate, he3nceit stops being an issue.

FRUIT SUGARS

Another frequently asked question is, "Are fruits bad for you?" Most people recognize that fruits have sugar within them. However, this sugar is *natural fructose*. When natural sugars (in fruits and vegetables) are ingested, the release of converted complex sugars is much slower, and require less of an insulin response. This process should not provoke PMS symptoms.

It is important for every PMS woman to know that any particular food in general, but especially fruits, may act differently than expected. While one woman may have no problems eating fruits, another woman may find that eating fruits may in fact worsen her PMS symptoms. Each woman must test her own personal response to each individual food. If PMS symptoms are not affected or indeed disappear, then she is eating correctly. If on the other hand PMS symptoms persist or worsen, then she will have to reevaluate her choices. This concept should relate to all food, not just to sugars or complex carbohydrates.

ALCOHOL

We must address alcohol on its own. By alcohol we mean any wine, beer, and hard liquor, not to mention the mixers. Not only does alcohol have a refined sugar action, but it also has specific problems of its own. In the PMS woman, alcohol can temporarily relieve PMS symptoms.

Alcohol acts like a sudden infusion of sugar, causing the blood sugar level to rise. However, this rise docs not last very long and may drop away rapidly. Another drink is often required to recapture the desired effects. Alcohol, however, has addicting qualities, so it is common to see women who were initially drinking alcohol to relieve their PMS symptoms, end up becoming alcoholics.

This mechanism may be responsible for substantial numbers of women who have become alcoholics. Alcohol, in itself, is well known to produce deficiencies in magnesium and the

30 Days To No More PMS
The Cook Book

B-complex vitamins, thus potentiating the PMS and worsening the whole process.

CHAPTER 3

ELIMINATING PMS THROUGH THE FOODS YOU EAT

PMS AND THE FOODS YOU EAT

The most important concept to remember about PMS is, your diet will determine whether you have PMS symptoms or not. The types of foods you eat, or don't eat, ultimately determine whether you have dietary deficiencies or not. The specific deficiencies, (magnesium and vitamin B6) and excesses (refined sugars, caffeine) are generally responsible for the types of symptoms you experience, their intensity and their severity. The best way to control, and eventually eliminate PMS, is through your diet.

> **The Types of Foods You Eat, or Don't Eat, Ultimately Determine Whether You Have Dietary Deficiencies or Not.**

To get the best results, it is essential to choose foods that will replenish your vitamin-mineral stores and reverse the nutritional deficiency process. The following points outline the factors you will have to consider when making food choices.

You must choose those foods that will:

1. Not make your PMS worse.
2. Provide sufficient nutrients (magnesium and B6, etc.) needed to eliminate your symptoms.
3. Balance any hidden deficiencies or offending substances in your diet.
4. Provide, along with vitamin-mineral supplements, sufficient quantities of the essential nutrients necessary to keep you symptom free.
5. Prevent you from ever having PMS in the future.

To rephrase what we have said above:

What You Used to Eat Caused Your PMS - What You Choose to Eat Now Can Eliminate It!

30 Days To No More PMS
The Cook Book

An appropriate *Anti-PMS Diet* must provide an adequate amounts of the nutrients that will and can prevent PMS as well as make your body more efficient in its metabolic processes.

> *What You Used to Eat Caused Your PMS - What You Choose to Eat Now Can Eliminate It!*

To fully understand the effects of dietary deficiencies on your body we offer the following example:

> If you have ever fueled your car with a lower than recommended octane gasoline you may have observed what happened to the vehicle's performance. It probably pinged, sputtered and lacked pick-up; it may have chugged up hills instead of cruising smoothly. It may have even died out a number of times. In short, the vehicle lost performance. You, as the driver (or passenger) could easily feel this happening. This is what happens in PMS. If you ingest a poor quality fuel (inappropriate or deficient foods) you may get *symptoms* of PMS. It is just that simple.

You, of course, are not a car and you do not ingest a single, easy to identify fuel. The fuels you consume are complex and varied. They change from meal to meal and day to day. Since you have no owner's manual to tell you what you should or should not be eating, you may feel that you have little control over your PMS. You may, in fact, feel as if you are a victim of PMS. But this is not true, you are only a victim if you keep making the dame mistakes.

The treatment for PMS is almost as simple as the treatment used to bring your car back to normal. Merely by changing the type of fuel back to the higher octane, the car's performance problems disappear. With PMS you do exactly the same thing. When you change your diet to foods containing higher amounts of magnesium and vitamin B6, and decrease the poorer quality foods such as refined and processed foods (high calcium foods, simple sugar and caffeine) your symptoms have no further reason to exist. The better you get at choosing your foods, the fewer symptoms you will experience. By doing this you enhance your body's overall performance.

30 Days To No More PMS
The Cook Book

THE BASICS STEPS TO SUCCESSFUL ELIMINATION OF PMS

The first step in mastering PMS is to learn all about it, its theories, its causes and the available methods of treatment. We have provided this information for you in our 30 Days To No More PMS, A Doctor's Proven Nutritional Program. Next is choosing a method of treatment. If you have decided to choose the nutritional approach to relieve your symptoms, then we commend you for your choice. This means that you will have started on the right path to getting well. Congratulations. If you chose medical or hysterectomy (which would be done only if you have other medical problems that would justify this major surgical procedure) consider changing your diet as well, to maximize your results.

In the chapters above, we have reviewed this basic information necessary for you to be successful in controlling and even eliminating all of your PMS symptoms. In this next chapter will explain how to use this information and exactly what is needed to make the dietary approach work. Before going any farther we suggest you study Table 5, below. This Table summarizes the *basic rules* of the anti-PMS diet.

To reduce or eliminate your PMS symptoms it will be important to have a steady flow of essential anti-PMS nutrients. We have already discussed several reasons for this. One of the primary problems PMS women face is low blood sugar (hypoglycemia, from Dr. Abraham's PMS-C symptom group: headaches, increased appetite, cravings, heart pounding, fatigue, lightheadedness, etc.) Eating six times a day can reduce these symptoms. The body's need for magnesium to appropriately process estrogen also requires a fairly constant flow of this mineral into your system.

MAKING THE ANTI-PMS DIET WORK FOR YOU

Let's first start first with an overview of the general PMS Nutritional Guidelines:

1. Eating three modest meals and two to three snacks each day. Therefore, start by cutting out all large meals. Once again this is done to present your body with essentially nutrients all through the day so that you do not become deficient nor develop hypoglycemia. Estimate the amounts and portions you would normally eat throughout any single day, then divide this amount into 3 modest meals and two to three snack portions. You can use the section on menu planning in Section II, Chapter 2 to assist you in doing this.

2. It is important not to skip meals. We realize that many women skip meals because they worry

30 Days To No More PMS
The Cook Book

that they will gain weight. Remember, when you are not eating, your body is not getting the necessary nutrients and you are essentially worsening your PMS. We realize that asking you to eat six small meals a day requires a giant leap of faith on your part. However, most women who learn to eat this way control their appetite better, eat healthier foods and most have actually lost weight. Most women soon find that their body actually needs to be fed every 3-4 hours. By combining whole grains, fresh vegetables, ad fresh fruits, some nuts, along with small portions of poultry or fish and then dividing them up into smaller, easier to eat portions, PMS symptoms are improved. Women also find that they are less hungry, cravings are reduced or eliminated, digestion is improved and they actually feel and look better[6].

3. Dividing meals into smaller portions and having nutritious snacks between meals will change the flow of energy in your system. However, by itself this is not enough. The most important of these steps is to increase foods that are high in magnesium. This is done by increasing high magnesium foods, once again: whole grains, vegetables, nuts and fruits. We will describe an easy way of doing this in the next section based on the food lists provided in Appendices 2 and 3.

4. Many women have the mistaken idea that complex carbohydrates, whole grain breads and cereals, beans, fruits and even starchy vegetables are somehow more fattening than other foods. This is entirely wrong. In reality these categories of foods, proteins, and carbohydrates each provide 4 calories per gram to our diet. Fats provide 8 calories per gram, while alcohol provides 9 calories per each gram you eat or drink. Proteins and carbohydrates (fruits, vegetables and starches) all provide the exact same number of calories per gram. Fats, on the other hand, have twice the number of calories as protein and carbohydrates. Red meats contain both protein and fat and therefore are relatively higher in calories than grains, fruits and vegetables which have little or no fats. Since grains, vegetables and fruits have very little fat and sometimes, even no fat so they are, unit for unit, much lower in calories and therefore less fattening. In order to reduce foods with a high fat content, it will be important to change your sources of proteins from red meats to chicken, turkey, fish, legumes (beans) and nuts and increase the amounts of complex carbohydrates in your diet. (For information on fats see Appendix 6 and for weight loss, see Appendix 8). The difference between refined and processed foods, and whole fresh foods are that during the refining process many vitamins, minerals and fiber are removed so that the calories they contain are now without the essential nutrients needed by your body. This is why we call these foods *empty-calorie foods.* While they have calories, they little or no, or certainly less, essential nutrients than their original fresh whole food brothers and sisters. This means that while you may pay less for them, you will also

30 Days To No More PMS
The Cook Book

get much less nutritional value for your money. In one sense, they are depleted of nutrition and when you are eating them you are further depleting your body's stores of essential nutrients needed to metabolize them. To add insult to injury, weight gain is much more likely to occur with eating empty-calorie foods as compared to eating whole foods. Finally, when you eat empty-calorie foods you are actually starving your body as most have little or no essential nutrients which your body desperately needs to maintain your good health and well-being.

5. Since most foods that have elevated magnesium content also are high in vitamin B6, choosing foods specifically for their B6 and other B vitamins is generally unnecessary. If any reader is specifically interested, Appendices 9 and 10 list foods high in specific B vitamins. Also remember, when you cook foods B vitamins are either destroyed by the heat or leached into the water the food is cooked in. B vitamins are best obtained from fresh raw foods (whole grains, vegetables and fruits).

6. While working at increasing magnesium rich foods, it is also necessary to limit foods containing large amounts of calcium (See Appendix 3). This included dairy products, cheeses and packaged or prepared products that contain milk and dairy products. Remember as we have repeatedly stated, this does not mean that you will eliminate *all* calcium from your diet. This can't be done without an enormous amount of effort. Calcium is found in most foods, especially, much to the chagrin of the PMS woman, most of the foods she usually likes to eat (Remember, you wouldn't have PMS if they weren't.) Generally the easiest thing to do is to not worry about calcium in vegetables but chose foods that will increase the magnesium to calcium ratio *of the foods you ultimately choose to eat*, and these steps are explained in greater detail in the remainder of this section.

7. The next important step is to eliminate as many foods as possible refined and processed foods especially those that contain refined sugars (See Chapter 3 and Appendix 7), bleached flours and processed grains and cereals. In order to do this you will have to start reading food-product labels before you purchase foods at the market. Cutting out processed or junk foods' means eliminating **ALL** products from your diet that either do not contain whole grains or that have sugar added to it. Since this is an important step and must be given your highest priority.

The next step is to *eliminate* caffeine rich foods (See Appendix 4) from your diet. This can be difficult or easy depending on whether you are addicted to caffeine. If you drink large amounts of caffeinated coffee or soft drinks, you may not be able to just *cut them out*. You may have to withdraw yourself over a period of time. Some women have withdrawal symptoms when trying

30 Days To No More PMS
The Cook Book

to eliminate caffeine. If this should happen to you, we suggest that you withdraw slowly enough to eliminate withdrawal symptoms. You may substitute decaffeinated coffee for regular coffee, you may mix equal parts of decaf and regular coffee or alternate decaf and regular. Whatever you need to do to get off caffeine is probably all right as long as you eliminate it from your diet.

GENERAL PMS DIETARY (NUTRITIONAL) GUIDELINES

1. Eat 6 (six) small meals rather than 2 or 3 large meals each day.

2. 60-70% of daily calories should come from complex carbohydrates (grains, legumes and cereals).

3. Use fish, poultry, whole grains and legumes as your major sources of protein. Consume *no more than* 3 oz. of red meats per week.

4. Limit dairy products to *no more than* 2 (two) servings per week (8 oz. milk or 2 oz. cheese = 1 serving).

5. Limit refined sugar to *no more than* 5 tsp. per day. Refined sugar = white sugar, honey, brown sugar, turbinado or raw sugar, molasses, sucrose, lactose, dextrose, maltose, fructose, corn syrup and sweetener.

6. Limit alcohol consumption to *no more than* 1 oz. per week if at all.

7. Do *not* over salt foods. Rather than cooking with salt add to taste afterward.

8. Use corn margarine or safflower oil margarine instead of butter.

9. *Avoid* processed foods or bleached/white flours and grains as they provide empty calories and may be metabolized as simple carbohydrates.

10. Use 1 tbsp. cold pressed safflower oil each day as a source of cis-linoleic acid. This is especially valuable for women who have problem menstrual cramping.

11. Drink *at least* 4-6 (8 oz.) glasses of water each day or more.

12. Most important *eliminate* caffeine rich foods and drinks (coffee, tea, colas and chocolates).

Table 5

30 Days To No More PMS
The Cook Book

SELECTING FOODS TO EAT

In this section and the next we will begin to help you choose good healthful, even delicious foods, which can help you eliminate your PMS.

There is no question in our minds that you must enjoy what you eat. The foods you choose must be easily available and otherwise nutritious. Without question there will be no problems meeting these needs. You should never choose foods that you don't like to eat for if you do you will be unhappy. On the other hand, you may want to retry foods that you had passed judgement on years ago when you were a child or without a fair trial. We encourage you to be adventurous and consider foods and combinations of foods that previously you might not have wished to explore. Often women tell us that they were happy that they did try foods they had previously "misjudged."

In the remainder of this chapter we will tell you how to use the food lists in Appendices 2 and 3 to choose foods that will assist you in eliminating your PMS symptoms.

USING THE FOOD LISTS

Familiarize yourself with the food lists in Appendices 2 and 3. First, look through Appendix 2, High Magnesium Foods. Notice how may foods from this list you eat frequently. If there are quite a few foods you eat and enjoy, it is likely that your PMS problems are caused by a relative deficiency.

In this case, you will need to evaluate your diet for excess calcium, simple carbohydrates and caffeine. With the information we have already given you and the information in Appendices 3, 4, 5, 7 and 9 you should be able to determine which foods will work to relieve your symptoms and which foods will worsen your symptoms. Now make your own lists of "good" and "not so good" foods based on these new criteria.

If you find that you eat very few foods from the high magnesium list, it is likely you have an absolute deficiency. In this case, start by choosing as many high magnesium foods as you can, then work them into your meal plan look for the Meal Plan Form in the Forms Section at the back of this book. Remember. It is in your best interest to eat every three to four hours. Each small meal or snack should have a high magnesium food so that you have a relatively constant flow of magnesium into your system throughout the day. Your goal is to create menus which allow at least twice as many milligrams of magnesium as calcium, preferably a 2 to 1 ratio.

30 Days To No More PMS
The Cook Book

Appendices 2 and 3 are each set up so you can pick from the different food groups. First, pick foods from those groups highest in magnesium or lowest in calcium. You will ideally take in at least 300 mg to 600 mg of magnesium daily. Start at the low end to avoid loose bowel movements or diarrhea. As your system adjusts, increase the amount you take in each day. A daily intake below 300 mg may not be sufficient to relieve your symptoms.

As you look at Appendix 3, the Foods to Avoid list, you will probably notice immediately that this list is much larger than the High Magnesium list. Again, this is one of the reasons for PMS; there are many more high calcium foods than high magnesium foods. You should also notice that this list is set up differently from the magnesium list. It has calcium levels in the first column to allow you to see which foods have a higher calcium to magnesium ratio. Each succeeding entry has less calcium and more magnesium. It is best to reduce or eliminate these high calcium to magnesium foods during the premenstrual phase.

Eventually, you will reach a group of foods labeled, Neutral Foods. These foods all have ratios of magnesium to calcium which are less than 2 to 1. Unless your symptoms are extremely difficult to manage, you can essentially eat all you want of these foods. They will neither worsen nor improve your symptoms. If you are sensitive and have difficulty managing your symptoms, choose the higher magnesium foods rather than the higher calcium foods.

In all three lists, High Magnesium Foods, High Calcium Foods and Neutral Foods, we have given the specific amounts of magnesium and calcium[7] as well as the ratios of magnesium to calcium (Mg/Ca). These provide an instant way of evaluating each food as to whether it will give you a 2 to 1 Mg/Ca ratio for your diet. You will notice that throughout the lists the ratios do not take into consideration the total amount of each substance. For example, one food might have 4 mg of magnesium and 2 mg of calcium. This food therefore has a 2:1 Mg\Ca ratio. Another food may have 200 mg of magnesium and 100 mg of calcium. This food also has a ratio of 2:1 Mg/Ca. While the first food has only 4 mg of magnesium, the second food has 200 mg. Which food will be better for you? Both are good, but they just have different amounts of magnesium and calcium. If you need a higher amount of magnesium quickly, the 200-mg food will do this. However, you will also get 100 mg of calcium with it. The first food is negligible in both magnesium and calcium so you could essentially eat as much as you want. Both foods will only end up maintaining the Mg/Ca ratio where it is. To ultimately keep total calcium levels down you will want to make sure that you pick plenty of foods where the ratio of mg to ca is greater than 2:1.

30 Days To No More PMS
The Cook Book

PICKING YOUR FOODS

    Rule Number One: Eat only foods you like.
    Rule Number Two: Learn to like the foods that are most healthy for you.
    Rule Number Three: Forget rule one, until you are symptom free.

In order to get symptom free you may have to be adventurous and try foods you previously had biases against. If you look at the food lists and tell yourself that you are not interested, or don't like the majority of foods, the dietary program will not work for you.

We want you to have a large variety of foods to choose from anytime you need them. Between the food lists, the hints and recipes we have given you, you should find many ways to get the nutrients you need to help eliminate your PMS.

TAKE YOUR TIME

As we said above, take your time and learn to recognize the foods that are good for you as well as those that will potentially worsen you symptoms. Make your own list to carry in your purse. This will enable you to have a list of your high magnesium and high calcium foods available whenever or wherever you need them.

We often have women tell us that they should not be having problems with PMS because they eat very well. Let's look at an average meal. To help you understand how to pick food, we would like to run through several examples to demonstrate to you how to select foods that will eliminate your PMS.

EXAMPLE #1

How about a nice, green salad, with lots of carrots, cucumbers, some beautiful ripe tomatoes, some delicious low-fat mozzarella cheese and to top it off, a low-fat Italian dressing. A nice lunch, wouldn't you say? Low calorie, low fat, plenty of fiber. Sounds good, doesn't it? But us it going to decrease or increase your PMS symptoms?

Let's look at its makeup in relation to PMS; especially its calcium and magnesium content:

30 Days To No More PMS
The Cook Book

	Calcium	Magnesium	Mg/Ca Ratio
Lettuce, Romaine, 3½ ounces	68 mg.	11 mg.	0.2
Carrot, 1 medium, raw	19 mg.	11 mg.	0.6
Cucumber, ½ cup sliced	7 mg.	6 mg.	0.9
Mozzarella cheese, part skim	207 mg.	7 mg.	0.03
Tomato, ½ raw	4 mg.	7 mg.	1.8
Italian dressing, 2 tbsp.	4 mg.	2 mg.	0.5

Now let's add it all up:

The salad as it is above contains:	309 mg.	44 mg.	0.14

...and

How about some Rye Krisp crackers?	2 mg.	8 mg.	4.0

This salad may look good and even taste good, but it will not help you to eliminate your PMS. In fact it may make it worse.

"Well," you say, "what if we eliminate the cheese, after all cheese is dairy and dairy is higher in calcium, isn't it?" You are exactly right so let's see what happens when we do this.

	Calcium	Magnesium	Mg/Ca Ratio
The salad with cheese contains	309 mg.	44 mg.	0.14
Mozzarella cheese, part skim	-207 mg.	-7 mg.	0.03
The salad without the cheese	**102 mg.**	**37 mg.**	**0.4**

Well, that helped, a little, but the mozzarella also has some magnesium so it didn't help really all that much, did it? We did increase the Mg/Ca ratio from 0.14 to 0.4, a definite improvement, but not one that is going to help us very much.

30 Days To No More PMS
The Cook Book

How about if we leave the cheese out but add 2 nice rye krisp crackers to the lunch?

	Calcium	Magnesium	Mg/Ca Ratio
The salad without the cheese contains:	102 mg.	37 mg.	0.4
2 Rye krisp crackers	24 mg.	68 mg	2.8
Total Lunch: Salad and Rye Krisp	**126 mg.**	**105 mg.**	**0.8**

Well, this helped a bit more, but we are still not anywhere near 2.0 or more where we will be getting help for your PMS.

If we analyze this carefully, we'll find that this meal has 1.2 times as much calcium as magnesium. (The Mg/Ca ratio is 0.8, we want to go to 2.0 at least hence we still need to more than double the total amount of magnesium without changing the amount of calcium, this is not going to happen easily.) This meal would not help you treat your PMS. Now can you see why it is so easy to eat yourself into PMS. Notice that this meal is not a bad meal. Almost anyone would tell you that this is an extremely healthy way of eating, except if you are trying to avoid PMS.

EXAMPLE #2

Now let's add some more high magnesium food to this meal. We will add more foods from the Desired Foods List. Let's look at the Desired Foods List and see if you can find some foods which are relatively high in magnesium (and of course, vitamin B6). There are a number of foods which we can add into our lunch and can be eaten along with the salad which will immediately increase the amount of magnesium.

Let's trade the mozzarella for something else, for example, avocado, cashews, peanut butter, baked potato or corn on the cob.

	Calcium	Magnesium	Mg/Ca Ratio
Salad without cheese	102 mg.	37 mg.	0.4

30 Days To No More PMS
The Cook Book

Avocado California, 1 medium	19 mg.	70 mg.	3.7
Total for Lunch & Mid Afternoon Snack	**121 mg.**	**107 mg.**	**0.88**

Notice now that the calcium has increased only slightly but the magnesium has more than doubled. The amount of calcium is now just a fraction above 1.13 times as much magnesium. The Mg/Ca ratio is now 0.88. This meal is moving more toward neutral rather than PMS provoking.

EXAMPLE #3

In the process of increasing magnesium and making this meal a better anti-PMS meal, let's add a side of black beans. Sound good? Watch and see how you can eat yourself out of PMS and love it.

	Calcium	Magnesium	Mg/Ca Ratio
Salad with avocado & rye krisp	**121 mg.**	**107 mg.**	**0.88**
With a side of black beans	47 mg.	121 mg.	2.6
Total for Lunch	**168 mg.**	**228 mg.**	**1.4**

We have now reversed the Mg/Ca ratio and have more magnesium than calcium. While we still do not have a great deal of magnesium in this meal, we are far ahead of what we started with, in the beginning. This one meal isn't going to solve your PMS problem, but at this point it won't make your PMS worse. Now in the next set of examples let's see how we can get you to a 2 to 1 or better ratio through the remainder of the meals and snacks of the day.

EXAMPLE #4

If you were to have a mid-afternoon snack of 1 ounce of dry roasted cashews, you will further increase the magnesium total for the whole day.

	Calcium	Magnesium	Mg/Ca Ratio

30 Days To No More PMS
The Cook Book

Lunch	168 mg.	228 mg.	1.4
Cashews (1 oz., dry roasted), a snack	13 mg.	74 mg.	5.7
Total Lunch plus Snack	**181 mg.**	**302 mg.**	**1.7**

The numbers are now getting better and better. We are now at 302 mg. of magnesium and your Mg/Ca ratio is now at 1.7. This is mid-neutral, not worsening and possibly lessening your PMS symptoms.

EXAMPLE #5

Now let's look at dinner:

	Calcium	Magnesium	Mg/Ca Ratio
Baked potato, one medium	22 mg.	54 mg.	2.5
Turkey, white meat, 3 oz.	6 mg.	15 mg.	2.5
Peas and carrots, 1/4 cup, steamed	8 mg.	26 mg.	3.3
Total Lunch	**36 mg.**	**95 mg.**	**2.6**
Add to Lunch and Snack above	181 mg.	302 mg.	1.7
Total Lunch & Dinner	**217 mg.**	**397 mg.**	**1.8**

Now you're at a total of 397 mg. of magnesium and a Mg/CA ratio of 1.8. We have moved forward but we're still not at the 2:1 ratio. However, we have forgotten all about breakfast today. So let's go back and look at what you could have eaten for breakfast.

EXAMPLE #6

If, at breakfast you had eaten a bowl of oatmeal fortified with some rice bran, your outlook might well be entirely different at this point.

	Calcium	Magnesium	Mg/Ca Ratio

30 Days To No More PMS
The Cook Book

Oatmeal, Quick, ¾ cup	15 mg.	42 mg.	2.8
½ Tbsp. Rice Bran	10 mg.	160 mg.	16.0
Add Ex. 3, 4 and 5 above	217 mg.	397 mg.	1.8
Total All Meals for the Day	**242 mg.**	**599 mg.**	**2.5**

Now, the total amount of magnesium for the day is 599 mg. and the Mg/Ca ratio, is at 2.5 magnesium to 1 calcium. Your diet for this day would not only reduce your symptoms but even help eliminate them.

EXAMPLE #7

We still want you to have a morning snack, for that is extremely important in order to maintain an even blood sugar level, giving you energy and managing your PMS:

For your morning snacks let's have:

	Calcium	Magnesium	Mg/Ca Ratio
Banana, 1 medium	7 mg.	33 mg.	4.7
Apple juice, 8 oz., frozen or fresh	14 mg.	12 mg.	0.9
Add Ex. 3-6 above	242 mg.	599 mg.	2.5
Total All Meals & Snacks for the Day	**263 mg.**	**644 mg.**	**2.5**

Your total magnesium is now 644 mg, and while mg/Ca Ratio is still only 2.5 which is well within the upper range of helping to resolve PMS symptoms, we have added more sugar to your system to fight hypoglycemia and to maintain a relatively even blood sugar.

While the morning or afternoon snacks don't always substantially change the Mg/Ca ratio, they do help maintain adequate daily blood sugar, as well as helping to maintain a constant flow of magnesium into the body.

30 Days To No More PMS
The Cook Book

SUCCESS IN YOUR GRASP

At first making changes in your diet may feel somewhat uncomfortable. However, if you can keep in mind how much you want to eliminate your PMS symptoms, these changes will become much easier. It is also helpful to remember our credo "What you used to eat caused your PMS, what you choose to eat now can eliminate it." Some foods will be more difficult to give up than others. If your discomfort with PMS is great and your desire to eliminate your symptoms is strong, you **must** continue to work on your diet to eliminate your symptoms.

> **What You Used to Eat Caused Your PMS,**
>
> **What You Choose to Eat Now**
>
> **Can Eliminate It.**

After a short time on this new diet, your negative and destructive cravings will begin to disappear and you will feel as if you are once again in control of your life. It won't take long before you discover that you really like what you are now eating. You no longer have to eat junk food just because everyone else is doing it. If you take advantage of the recipes and suggestions in part two of this book, you will soon be creating lots of healthful and delicious snacks and meals. Within a short time your symptoms will be gone and you will feel that your life is yours once again.

By balancing your small meals and snacks with correct food choices, you can enjoy the challenge of creating tasty high magnesium meals (See Section II, Chapter 1). Once you reach this level you will be able to maintain yourself entirely symptom free for the rest of your life.

CHEATING

Things that can interfere with your success are parties, dining out and old unbroken eating habits. Sometimes you may feel that you must join the crowd in eating foods, especially deserts, that you know you really shouldn't eat. Often special treats prepared by a friend or hostess at a dinner party are especially difficult to refuse. When eating out, it is always possible that there will be no "healthy" foods on the menu.

Sometimes, there really is a need to celebrate or to let go. We understand this. Many of our

30 Days To No More PMS
The Cook Book

patients have experienced this, even Lisa; after all we are only human. We refer to this brief detour from the diet as *cheating*. We do not do this to make you feel guilty. Rather, we do this to help you to put everything into its proper perspective, to help you most efficiently eliminate your PMS. You can best do this by following a well-crafted anti-PMS diet, all of the time. However, we realize that from time to time this will not always be practical nor possible, at certain times situations will arise that may take you away from your anti-PMS diet for a brief period of time. When this happens, if you don't know what to do it might throw you out of control for a while. However, you certainly don't have to become severely symptomatic. All you will ever need to do is go back on your anti-PMS dietary program.

To remain in control and keep yourself symptom free, you simply have to increase your magnesium and vitamin B6 intake (by either food or supplement, or both) either before or after you "cheat." In rare situations, if you really go way off of your dietary program, you might have to increase your high magnesium foods and vitamin-mineral supplements and even resort to natural progesterone for a while until you feel that you are back on track again. However, if you do cheat, don't think of yourself as a failure. Forgive yourself and get back on the program. Cheating us okay if you only do it for special events or when you have no other choice. But always remember to cover yourself (with high magnesium B6, foods and supplements) as best as you can when it is happening and to get back on the anti-PMS dietary program as soon as possible.

To help keep you from having to cheat when you are going to a party or a restaurant where you can't be assured of getting your high magnesium foods, eat before you go or take along high magnesium snacks. Planning ahead can insure your success.

USING SUPPLEMENTS TO GAIN AND MAINTAIN CONTROL

Once we started teaching the dietary approach to women, we recognized that PMS symptoms can vary widely from woman to woman. PMS is a spectrum of symptoms that range from very mild to extremely severe. One woman's symptoms may be better or worse than another is. We have observed that women who recognize and treat their symptoms early usually require much fewer dietary modifications. Often they may not even need vitamin-mineral supplements. On the other hand, women who wait until their symptoms are severe generally need much more rigid dietary control. These women benefit from using vitamin-mineral supplements and, on occasion, natural progesterone along with dietary modification.

30 Days To No More PMS
The Cook Book

Many women, especially those with moderate to severe PMS, may find that they must use vitamin-mineral supplements on a daily basis in order to gain control of their symptoms in the initial phases of treatment. Their bodies have existed in a state of deficit for so long that they are simply not able to consume sufficient magnesium and B6 to be able to rapidly transform the metabolic pathways back to their normal pre-PMS states. For these women, supplements are used simply as an additional food source. We instruct them not to think of their supplements as medicine but rather as food in a pill form. Continued use of supplements, along with diet modification, is usually necessary for most PMS women to remain asymptomatic for a while, however once she has established herself on her anti-PMS diet, supplements can be reduced and possibly even eliminated with the exception of when they are used to cover cheating.

SUMMARY OF THE ANTI-PMS DIET

The basis of the PMS diet is to replace all of the essential the vitamins and minerals needed, because your previous diet had been deficient. Having sufficient quantities of these nutrients enables your body to effectively regulate all biologic functions, and most important, to help regulate and normalize your estrogen and progesterone metabolism. Once you have returned to the right diet for you, the right ratio of estrogen to progesterone circulating within your body will normalize itself for your individual needs. Your PMS symptoms will then disappear. Because the body tries to be as efficient as it can it will create alternative and less effective metabolic pathways which lead to PMS symptoms. These alternative pathways may take time to return to normal. The more severe your PMS symptoms are, the greater the deficiencies the longer it will take and the more work you will have to do to rebalance your body.

Through this methodology you can take full control over your life. By using the 30 Days To No More PMS Dietary program, you can periodically go off of your diet (cheat) and then rapidly compensate for your actions. This often creates the best of all worlds for the PMS woman.

In women with mild PMS, dietary control may only be needed in the few days prior to the onset of PMS symptoms. Where PMS is severe, stricter dietary control may be needed for the entire month. Each woman must determine her exact needs based on how easily and rapidly her symptoms resolve.

The 30 Days To No More PMS anti-PMS diet is a superb and healthy diet. We suggest that you make it your diet of choice. When foods are picked thoughtfully, you can lose weigh, increase your energy, eliminate breast pain, eliminate swelling in upper and lower extremities, prevent

30 Days To No More PMS
The Cook Book

headaches, irritability and anxiety, diminish osteoporosis and prevent cardiovascular diseases. This diet can also reduce their risk of colon cancer and breast cancer.

"HOW WILL WE KNOW IF THE DIET IS WORKING?"

The answer to this question should be obvious by now. Your symptoms will disappear when you are on the *right* diet. That is, the *right* diet for *you*. If your symptoms are not eliminated, then *you* are not yet on the *right* diet *for your body's needs*.

"DO I HAVE TO GIVE UP ALL OF THE FOODS I LIKE?" (Milk, Cheeses, Ice Cream, Cakes, Cookies, Candies, Coffee and Soft Drinks.)
NO. You do not **have to** give up any of these foods at all. You can keep your PMS symptoms, if you so desire. If you want to eliminate of your PMS symptoms, you may have to alter the amount, timing and selection of the foods you eat until you find the right combination that allows you to have *no more PMS symptoms*.

"Is it really this Easy?" Yes and No! It can be easy or difficult. This depends totally on you. Your success will depend on how easily you can change how and what you eat. Here is a list of some of the many challenges you will likely face.

1. You may have to *re-evaluate* certain food prejudices.

2. You may have to *change* long-standing likes and dislikes.

3. You may have to *eliminate* certain food addictions (usually PMS-producing foods).

4. You will have to *learn* which foods and substances are inherently good and which are not so good for you. This, of course, is what 30 Days To No More PMS, A Doctor's Proven Nutritional Program - The Cook Book is about.

5. You may have to confront your *resistance* to change.

6. You will have to *give up secondary gains* in order to do away with PMS.

7. You will have to *develop a new sense of self-discipline* to make this diet work.

30 Days To No More PMS
The Cook Book

OTHER IMPORTANT AND VALUABLE FACTORS

Besides diet there are a number of other valuable things you can do that can do (See Table 6) help you to decrease the severity of your PMS symptoms. One of the most important factors appears to be exercise (See Chapter 6 in 30 Days To No More PMS, A Doctor's Proven Nutritional Program). Women who were previously sedentary may often significantly reduce their symptoms by exercising. Exercise burns circulating blood sugar. Exercise releases endorphins. It may well be that many of these women reduce sugars in their diet as well. Results may occur because new metabolic pathways are created which more effectively metabolize estrogen.

Whatever the mechanism, exercise is helpful and we recommend that women who desire relief from PMS create a safe exercise program for themselves. Cutting down or completely stopping smoking often helps to speed up relief of PMS symptoms.

Table 6 discusses other things you can do including getting more rest so that your body can function optimally, reducing stress, eliminating alcohol and smoking and keeping a daily diary to help you regulate both symptoms and diet. Personal Management Diary - Daily Symptoms Record Form which can be found in the Forms Section at the back of this book.

VALUABLE SUGGESTIONS

1. **EXERCISE** at least ½-hour each day. (Gardening, swimming or brisk walking of at least 4 to 5 miles per hour for 20 minutes, 3 times a week or more, or bicycling 20 minutes per day).

2. Get ample **SLEEP** and **REST** for your needs.

3. Schedule potentially **STRESSFUL** events at times other than during the premenstrual period when possible.

4. Keep a daily **DIARY** of your **SYMPTOMS** to help regulate the amount of supplements you need in order to be symptom free.

5. Limit **TOBACCO** use or stop entirely.

Table 6

30 Days To No More PMS
The Cook Book

AFFIRMATIONS CAN HELP

Affirmations are statements which we say and believe to reprogram our unconscious self. They are extremely helpful in speeding up relief of PMS symptoms. They can be used in the following way.

Each time you eat correctly (for you) and each time you take your vitamin-mineral supplements, repeat the following *affirmation*:

> **"I AM TAKING AN ACTIVE PART IN CREATING MY OWN
> GOOD HEALTH AND WELL BEING!
> I AM ELIMINATING MY PMS SYMPTOMS!"**

SUMMARY

We wish that women never had to experience PMS. However, PMS does exist and we have learned that you have two paths open to you, you can either let PMS control you or you can take control of your PMS. Most women choose to take control of their PMS. By changing your diet as we have described above, you can master your PMS and your symptoms. You can once again be in charge of your own life.

When you are once again back at the control panel of your body, you will never want to go back to the old Jekyll and Hyde self again. We invite every PMS sufferer to join the thousands of women who have conquered it and have NO MORE PMS!

CHAPTER 4

SUPPLEMENTS AND HOW TO USE THEM

WHAT SUPPLEMENTS ARE RECOMMENDED?

There are now a number of fine vitamin-mineral supplements that are balanced specifically for women and the treatment of PMS. These are best found at quality pharmacies and health food stores. In order for any product to relieve PMS symptoms it must meet two major criteria. First, the formulation must contain between 200 mg and 400 mg of magnesium or more. Second, it must have no greater than 200 mgs of Calcium per daily dosage. Third, the most valuable products will have a minimum of a 2:1 ratio of magnesium to calcium and preferably even 3:1 or 4:1 Mg/Ca.

A good product should also contain a full complement of all of the B vitamins with at least 100% of the RDA (Recommended Dietary Allowance). It certainly can have more than the RDA amounts as long as all of the B vitamins listed in Appendix 9 are present. Supplements with higher than the RDA amounts of calcium, magnesium, B and other vitamins and minerals are generally referred to as mega-vitamin dosages.

ARE THERE DANGERS TO MEGA-DOSE VITAMIN THERAPY SUPPLEMENTS?

Yes and No! Like anything else, a little bit may be good and a lot may be dangerous. The formulas should be within what is generally considered safe levels and used as directed. Toxicity may occur with certain vitamins if used in large, unsupervised doses. Vitamins A, D and E are well known to be fat soluble and therefore can be stored in the body's fat tissues. If taken for a long period of time in excessive doses, toxicity can occur. (See Vitamin Toxicity - Table 7)

Recently, Vitamin B6 has been found to have toxicity symptoms when taken in massive doses. B6 should never be taken alone. It should be in a balanced B-Complex formula with magnesium and other essential minerals. Vitamin B6, when taken alone, especially in large amounts, may create temporary relief of PMS symptoms. However, it will require progressively larger doses to continue and to maintain these results. This process can ultimately lead to ingesting extremely high levels of B6 which can easily reach toxic levels.

30 Days To No More PMS
The Cook Book

	Vitamin Toxicity
Vitamin A:	100,000 IU per day for any period of time, possibly grater than one to two months, can lead to toxic symptoms.
Vitamin D:	100,000 IU has been noted as top level above which there generally is not benefit. Toxicity may be in the range of 300,000 IU per day for more than 1 to 3 months.
Vitamin E:	Therapeutic doses of vitamin V range from 300 to 2,000 IU per day. Toxicity occurs in only two groups of people 1) high blood pressure patients 2) chronic rheumatic heart disease patients.
Vitamin B6:	Toxicity has been reported with doses in excess of 200 mg per day for several months.

Table 7

HOW DO I KNOW WHICH VITAMINS TO TAKE?

There is only one way to know, by the results you get. If you merely go to your local health food store, you will be deluged by a mountain of products. You may find it hard to get just the right combination vitamins and minerals that *will work* to eliminate your PMS symptoms. It would help if you knew not only about formulations but about chelation, absorption, interactions, competition and other important aspects of vitamins and minerals. When not fully understood, even experts may believe that vitamins don't work. A simple solution is to choose a PMS nutritional supplement which already has correct magnesium to calcium ratio, the correct amount of vitamin B6 and a complete balance of all other essential vitamins and minerals. These products usually clearly indicate on their label the number of tablets required to get desired results. Any woman can then easily regulate the number of tablets taken along with a healthy anti-PMS diet to get complete symptom relief without toxicity.

HOW DO I KNOW HOW MANY VITAMINS TO TAKE?

We usually suggest that you start the first day with a quarter of the dosage recommended on the label. Continue this until you feel entirely comfortable, or until you are ready to go to the next highest dosage level. Add one tablet daily or every other day until your system is used to the vitamin-mineral preparation. Through this method you should be able to increase the dosage slowly and steadily until you reach the therapeutic dosage recommended for that particular

30 Days To No More PMS
The Cook Book

preparation. If you start out with too much, you may become nauseated or even vomit. You may get a bad taste in your mouth and feel uncomfortable or fatigued. Sometimes this can also be caused by taking vitamins on an empty stomach. Remember, vitamins are food supplements and work best when taken with food.

The total amount of any vitamin-mineral supplement you take will depend on the severity of your PMS symptoms, your tolerance to the supplement and its ingredients, the recommended safe dosage and the result you desire. You can use your PEQ scores to determine the approximate amount you will need for complete symptom relief. Without trained help, however, you will have to use the process of trial and error to determine your specific needs. It is most important that you follow this manual and the directions on the package, and that you do not exceed the daily recommended amounts.

WHAT KIND OF PREPARATION SHOULD I HAVE BEFORE TREATING MY PMS?

You should have a complete *physical examination* which includes an evaluation of your heart, lungs, blood pressure, liver and kidneys. It is important to have a pelvic examination and pap smear to evaluate for cancer, uterine size, fibroid tumors, endometriosis and ovarian tumors. You should have a breast exam not only to evaluate for cancer but for fibrocystic disease of your breasts. Blood tests for anemia, blood cancer, diabetes, thyroid, liver and kidney function should be run. Hormonal studies are rarely necessary as they are too insensitive at this time to pick up the estrogen-progesterone defect. Cholesterol, HDL and LDL fractions as well as triglycerides may be helpful in evaluating your *cardio-vascular status* for prevention of atherosclerosis.

Dietary analysis is extremely helpful in evaluating your present diet which created your PMS. The analysis can determine your calcium and magnesium intake and probably more important your sugar intake (especially what is hidden and unknown). Caffeine, additives and fats in your diet should also be evaluated.

Hair analysis, considered controversial in its value, may have a place in comparing your daily dietary intake with hair content. Although still a new field, this can frequently add valuable information in otherwise extremely difficult, resistant or complicated situations.

Remember to approach the treatment of your PMS symptoms wisely. Choose the medical consultant who best represents your views. Do not criticize or think

30 Days To No More PMS
The Cook Book

of yourself as a failure, if you do not get immediate results. You may find that to be successful you may just need to try a different approach. Consider your diet first as the major culprit in causing PMS.

SECTION II

ANTI-PMS RECIPES

30 Days To No More PMS
The Cook Book

(This Page Is Purposefully Left Blank For You To Use To Take Notes)

CHAPTER 1

DELICIOUS ANTI-PMS FOODS

STARTING YOUR ANTI-PMS DIET

You are now ready to put the 30 Days To No More PMS Dietary program into action. In this section we have many recipes and suggestions for healthful and nutritious eating. We are including everything from snacks to main courses, deserts and even drinks. You may combine these dishes in any way you like into meal plans for breakfast, midmorning snack, lunch, mid-afternoon-snack, dinner and late evening snack. Remember, it is important, at least in the beginning, to eat six (6) small meals a day. One way to do this is to take the normal amount of food you eat during a single day and breaking it up into six portions.

We know that every woman worries about gaining weight by eating frequently. This is a myth based on eating the wrong foods. If you eat low fat, high complex carbohydrates, eliminate junk foods which are nutritionally empty-calorie foods, reduce dairy and cheeses and excess salt, you will not gain weight, in fact you may either lose weight or find your normal weight and stay there. Only when you cheat with offender foods will you tend to gain weight.

Another important point is that you must like what you eat. If you don't, it will not necessarily satisfy you and you will eventually either overeat or stop eating the foods that can help you. In order for you to like what you are eating, you will have to select foods you enjoy and foods that support you. In order to do this, you may have to change your ideas about foods. Therefore, instead of simply eating for pleasure, see yourself eating to maintain your good health and well-being. Let food be secondary.

In order to do this you must strive to find and work at that which is in your highest and best interest. You must strive to become your highest and best self. Only when you are totally and completely you will you be totally and completely happy.

While what you eat is up to you, we suggest that you become as familiar as possible with the foods on the *Desired Foods* list in Appendix 2. Make a list of the foods which you enjoy most and feel most comfortable eating. You may then substitute these foods if you desire, simply by changing the recipes given below adding or subtracting good healthy anti-PMS foods. We suggest that you do vary your diet because if you don't vary what you eat, you may become bored with what you are eating and this might cause you to go off the anti-PMS diet and lose

30 Days To No More PMS
The Cook Book

all your good work.

SNACKS

Choosing snack foods which can help relieve PMS is extremely important. The rules are simple, stay away from foods high in sugar and simple carbohydrates, as well as foods loaded with calcium or salt. A good snack should not only help to curb your appetite, but it should also lessen your cravings for sweets and other less nutritional junk foods. Try some of the following recipes. They will help you to eat "right." Remember to always enjoy what you eat.

SNACK MIX
1 part plain Puffed Corn (No preservatives/No sugar)
1 part Puffed Wheat
1 part Puffed Rice

Pour the ingredients into a large container and mix. Keep this mixture on hand to insure you get the proper type of snack between meals and to keep your blood sugar stable.

HIGH ENERGY SNACK MIX
Use the basic SNACK MIX and add 1 cup of dry roasted peanuts, raw cashews, pecans or walnuts. (A favorite of ours is to make 1 cup assorted nuts.) To watch calories use the guide of 1 cup nuts to 3 cups SNACK MIX. This is especially helpful if there is a possibility of missing a meal.

FRUIT AND NUT SNACK MIX
Use the HIGH ENERGY SNACK MIX recipe and add Unsweetened dried banana chips. (Ingredients for this recipe are available at most health food stores.)

QUICK QUARTERS
2 RICE CAKES (Puffed rice compressed into thick crackers salted or unsalted it's up to you) or...

2 Whole grain crackers
1 tbsp Peanut Butter (slightly warmed to spread easily) OR...
1 tbsp Cashew Butter

30 Days To No More PMS
The Cook Book

Spread Peanut Butter on crackers and cut twice to create 4 rounded triangles, or 4 squares.

DOMINO QUARTERS
Use the basic QUICK QUARTERS recipe and cut ½ banana into slices place 2 or three slices onto each quarter.

SNOW CAPPED QUARTERS
Use the above recipes and add ½ tsp unsweetened grated coconut to top of each of the quarters.

EASY NO SUGAR GRANOLA
1 c. Buckwheat groats
1 c. Rolled oats or 1 c. Cornmeal
1 c. Bran flakes
½ c. Safflower oil, heated
½ c. Cashews, Raw, chopped
½ c. Peanuts, chopped
½ c. Almonds, chopped
¼ c. Sunflower seeds, hulled
¼ c. Sesame seeds
½ c. Dates, unsweetened, chopped
½ c. Banana chips, dried
½ c. Wheat germ flakes

Preheat oven to 300 degrees F. Stirring frequently, toast the above cereals, nuts and fruits in a 13 x 9 inch pan.

Toast in the following order:
1 c. Buckwheat groats for 10 minutes

Add and continue to stir;
1 c. Rolled oats or Cornmeal and 1 c. Wheat germ flakes and Bran flakes mixed with ½ c. heated Safflower oil. Continue to toast for 15 minutes.

Add:

30 Days To No More PMS
The Cook Book

Cashews, Peanuts, Almonds, Sunflower seeds and Sesame seeds. Stir and toast 10 more minutes. Remove from oven and add: Dates, Banana chips and Wheat germ.

AIR-POPPED POPPED CORN
½ c. Natural popping corn kernels
Pop in an Hot Air Popper.
Sprinkle lightly with curry powder or garlic powder.

TROPICAL FRUIT TREATS
Nectarines, bananas, mangoes, grapefruits or avocados can be eaten individually or in any combination you desire or choose to create for yourself. Watch the quantities you eat if you are counting calories.

APPETIZERS

These recipes can be used in small portions as appetizers or in larger portions as a main dish for one or two persons.

MARINATED MUSHROOMS
½ lb. Mushrooms, fresh with stems
¼ tsp. Salt or 1 tsp. Kikoman Soy Sauce
½ tsp. Oregano
3 tsp. Lemon juice
½ c. Safflower Oil (Cold Pressed)

Rinse and wipe mushrooms. Slice them evenly. Mix salt or soy sauce, oregano, lemon juice and safflower oil. Add to the mushrooms. Allow to stand at room temperature 2-3 hours or overnight. Yield: 3 Cups

GARLIC PEPPER MUSHROOMS
1 lb. Mushrooms, large, cleaned
2/3 c. Safflower Oil (Cold Pressed)
Juice of 2 Lemons
6 Peppercorns (whole)
1 Bay Leaf
2 Garlic Cloves

30 Days To No More PMS
The Cook Book

½ c. Water
½ tsp. Salt

Combine all ingredients except mushrooms in large saucepan. Cover and bring to a boil over medium heat. Reduce heat and simmer 15 minutes. Strain and return to saucepan. Add mushrooms and simmer 5 minutes, turning occasionally. Transfer to a bowl. Cover and chill. Yield: 2-3 Cups.

CLAM STUFFED MUSHROOMS
2 lbs. Medium Mushrooms (Approx 24)
1 Stick Safflower Margarine
3 Garlic cloves, minced
1 6 ½ or 8 oz. can Minced clams drained (save juice)
½ c. Bread crumbs (Whole Wheat)
¼ tsp. Freshly ground pepper
Salt to taste

Remove mushroom stems. Mince finely in blender or processor. Combine margarine and garlic in small saucepan and heat slowly until margarine is melted, stirring occasionally. Coat mushroom caps with mixture and set on baking sheet.

Preheat broiler. Combine clam juice and minced mushroom stems in small saucepan over medium heat and cook until tender. Add clams, bread crumbs, salt, pepper and heat thoroughly. Divide evenly among caps. Broil 6" from heat until lightly golden and heated thoroughly (about 5-8 minutes). Yield: 24 Stuffed Mushroom Caps.

MUSHROOM AND NUT PATE
¼ stick Safflower Margarine
1 lb. Mushrooms, sliced
1 Small Onion, sliced
1 clove Garlic, minced
3/4 c. Almonds slivered, toasted
¼ c. Cashews, toasted
2 tbsp. Safflower Oil

30 Days To No More PMS
The Cook Book

¼ tsp. Thyme, dried
Dash of Red pepper
Salt to taste

Melt butter in large skillet over medium high heat. Add mushrooms, onion and garlic. Saute until most of liquid has evaporated. Remove from heat.

Coarsely chop almonds and cashews in blender or food processor. Remove 2 tbsp. and set aside. Continue chopping, slowly adding oil until mixture is well blended. Add seasoning and mushroom mixture. Blend thoroughly. Stir in remaining nuts. Mold into loaf and sprinkle with shredded unsweetened coconut. Serve with assorted whole grain crackers. Yield: 6 servings.

CRAB STUFFED MUSHROOM CAPS
16 Mushrooms, size of silver dollar
½ c. Onion finely chopped
½ lb. lump Crabmeat
6 tbsp. Safflower Oil or Margarine
2 c. coarse Whole Wheat bread crumbs
Few drops of Lemon juice
1 tbsp. chopped Parsley
Salt and Pepper to taste

Preheat oven to 375 degrees. Wash mushrooms in cold water and remove all of the stems. Place mushroom caps in a bowl and sprinkle with few drops lemon juice.

Chop the mushroom stems finely and saute with onions in margarine. Cook until the onions are somewhat soft. Add crabmeat, bread crumbs, parsley, salt and pepper. Fold together well. Stuff the mushroom caps with the crabmeat mixture. Place on a baking tray and bake for 20 minutes. Yield: 2 Full meal servings or appetizers for 4-8.

SPICY GUACAMOLE
2 Avocado, very ripe
2 Tomatoes, medium

30 Days To No More PMS
The Cook Book

1 Onion, medium (or 1 bunch green onion) chopped
Salsa Jalapeno, or green peeled Chile
Rice vinegar or Lemon juice to taste
Salt to taste

Mash avocados with fork not too smooth, add other ingredients mix well. If not serving at once, cover tightly with plastic wrap. Yield: 3 Cups.

SHRIMP AND DIP
2-3 lbs. Shrimp, medium, raw
1 pint Homemade Oil Mayonnaise
½ tsp. Tabasco sauce
Juice of ½ Lemon
¼ c. Safflower Oil
½ stalk Celery, diced
1 tsp. Celery Seeds
1 Medium Onion, minced
Salt & Pepper to taste

One day before serving, cook shrimp in boiling water for 5 minutes or until they turn pink. Chill. Combine remaining ingredients and chill thoroughly. Place dip in serving bowl and surround with shrimp. Yield: 8-12 servings.

EGG NUT SPREAD
1 Hard-cooked Egg, grated
2 tbsp. chopped or ground Almonds (cashews, pecans or peanuts can be used)
1-2 tbsp. Homemade Oil Mayonnaise
Salt and Pepper to taste
Sliced Tomato (Optional)
Alfalfa Sprouts (Optional)

Combine egg, almonds & mayonnaise in a small bowl. Add salt & pepper to taste. Serve in a decorative bowl with whole grain crackers or cut up vegetables to dip in the mixture. Another way to serve this is to spread on whole grain bread, top with tomato and sprouts and top with second piece of whole grain bread. Cut into four small squares and serve. Yield: 2 Servings for sandwich or 8 squares.

30 Days To No More PMS
The Cook Book

ALFALFA SPROUT DIP OR SPREAD
1 c. Cashew butter
1/3 c. fresh Alfalfa Sprouts
Juice of 1 Lemon
¼ tsp. Salt
Dash Cayenne pepper

Blend ingredients together. Serve in a bowl with fresh sliced fruit, vegetables, whole grain crackers, or rice cakes for dipping. Yield: 1 1/3 Cups of dip.

SOUPS

For many of us, soups are a most enjoyable part of any meal. For many, it may be the meal, for soups often contain as many nutrients as an entire meal. For the PMS woman soups can be a source of instant relief from PMS symptoms, especially when it is designed to be high in magnesium and low in calcium.

CREAM OF CORN
2 c. Corn, fresh removed from the cob
2 c. Chicken stock
1 tbsp. Celery, chopped
1 tbsp. Onion, chopped
1 tsp. Worcestershire sauce
½ tsp. Celery salt
1 c. Milk
1 c. Potato, puree from fresh potatoes
Salt and Pepper

This soup is relatively high in magnesium. However, since it has 1 cup of milk in it and should be avoided by PMS women who have difficulty in controlling their symptoms.

Combine corn, chicken stock, celery, onions, Worcestershire sauce, and celery salt in a heavy pot or crock pot. Cover. Cook on a low flame. Puree in a blender. Return to pot. Add milk and pureed potato, salt and pepper. Heat until steaming. Serve in soup bowls. Garnish with air popped popcorn and almonds. Yield:

30 Days To No More PMS
The Cook Book

Serves 6.

POTATO SOUP
2 Potatoes, large, skinned and diced
1 c. Cauliflower, pureed
1 Onion, medium, chopped
3 stalks Celery, finely chopped with leaves
3 c. Chicken stock
1 Bay leaf
1 tsp. Margarine
Salt and Pepper

Saute' onions and celery in a heavy pot. Add into the pot potatoes, chicken stock and bay leaf. Cook until potatoes are tender. Cool briefly, then stir in a whisk the margarine and pureed cauliflower. Add salt and pepper to taste. Garnish with chives, green onion or dill. For variation add minced clams, carrots or whole cauliflower chunks.

LENTIL SOUPS
1 ½ c. Lentils, dried, presoaked and drained
1 Onion, medium, chopped
1 Carrot, skinned and grated
1 stalk Celery, chopped
3 tbsp. Safflower Oil
1 Bay leaf
2 cloves Garlic, minced
1 tsp. Salt
½ tsp. Oregano
½ c. Tomato sauce
3 tbsp. Red wine or rice vinegar
4 ½ c. Chicken stock

Simmer lentils in chicken stock for about 1 hour, or until almost tender. Saute' onions, carrots, and celery in oil until limp and glazed. Add this mixture to lentils. Add bay leaf, garlic, salt and oregano to the pot. Cover and cook on a low flame for 6 to 8 hours. Add tomato sauce and vinegar. Stir well. Cover and cook on high flame for 30 minutes or until flavors are well blended. Yield: 8 servings.

SWEDISH STYLE PEA SOUP
1 c. Yellow Split Peas
1 lb. Meat, cut in chunks (chicken, turkey or beef can be used)
2 qts. Water
½ tsp. Dry mustard
2 Carrots, skinned, diced
1 Onion, peeled, diced
Salt and Pepper

Soak peas and drain. Place in large heavy pot or crock pot; meat, water, mustard, carrots and onions. Cover and cook over a low flame for 8 to 12 hours, or until peas are tender. Remove meat. Place vegetables and pea broth in a blender, cover and blend until smooth. Return soup and diced meat to pot. Add salt and pepper to taste. Heat until steaming and serve. Yield: 8 servings.

VEGETABLE BARLEY MUSHROOM DELIGHT SOUP
2 c. Mushrooms, fresh sliced
¼ c. Carrots, diced
½ c. Onions, diced
½ c. Celery, diced
½ c. Barley
½ tsp. Marjoram
⅛ tsp. Pepper
½ tsp. Thyme
2 qts. Water, vegetable or chicken stock
¼ c. Safflower oil (optional if chicken stock is not used)
1 tsp. Salt

Saute' onions, carrots and celery in oil, covered, for 10 minutes. Add stock and bring to a boil. Add barley and return to a boil. Cover and turn down to a low simmer for 45 minutes. Add mushrooms, salt and other seasonings quickly, and continue to cook soup for another 45 minutes. Variation add 1 cup diced chicken or white meat turkey with the barley. Yield: 10 to 12 cups.

30 Days To No More PMS
The Cook Book

LIMA BEAN SOUP

½ c. Lima beans
4 c. Water or chicken stock
1 Bay leaf
3 or 4 Peppercorns
3 Whole cloves
1 Carrot, diced
3 stalks Celery, chopped with leaves
½ Onion, sliced
1 Garlic clove, minced
Salt and Pepper

Soak beans and drain. Add lima beans, water, bay leaf, peppercorns and cloves. Cook slowly until beans are soft, 2 ½ to 3 hours. In the last 30 minutes, add carrots, celery, onions, and garlic. Serve either as is or blend in blender. Variations: small amount of meat diced while cooking the soup remove prior to blending. Yield: 4 cups.

MULLIGATAWNY SOUP

1 c. Coconut, shredded
1 c. Boiling water
1 Onion, finely chopped
1 Carrot, grated
3 tbsp. Margarine
1 tbsp. Curry powder
1 Chicken, broiler-fryer, cut in pieces
2 Bay leaves
4 c. Chicken stock
Chopped cilantro to taste ¼ to ½ tsp.
Brown or wild rice, hot cooked, total amount depends on how much rice desired in each bowl. (See cooking instructions in grain section.)
1 medium Lime, cut in wedges

This is an Indian dish designed as a meal in itself.

Pour boiling water over coconut and let stand. Using a large frying pan, saute'

30 Days To No More PMS
The Cook Book

onions and carrots in margarine until limp and golden. Add curry powder. Cook 3 to 4 minutes. Add chicken and saute' until browned. Place in large heavy pot or crock pot. Drain coconut through wire strainer. Save liquid. Discard coconut. Add coconut liquid, stock and bay leaf to chicken. Season with salt and pepper. Cover pot, cook on high flame 2 to 3 hours, or until tender. Mound rice in bowls, ladle in soup. Serve with lime wedges. Yield: Serves 4 to 6.

VEGETABLE GUMBO SOUP
1 c. Corn, fresh
1 c. Lima beans
1 medium Onion, chopped
2 tbsp. oil
3 Cloves
1 Green pepper, diced
2 c, Tomatoes, diced
4 c. Vegetable stock
1 ½ c. Okra, sliced
1 tsp. Salt
¼ tsp. Allspice
½ c. Brown rice, cooked

Saute' onions and cloves in oil until the onions are soft. Remove the cloves Add green pepper and stir over a medium heat for several minutes. Then stir in the tomatoes. Bring the mixture to a boil, turn down the heat and let it simmer for 5 minutes. Add the rest of the ingredients. If using frozen okra, it should be at least partially thawed and then sliced. Bring the soup to a boil again, cover, and simmer for 15 minutes. Add rice. Yield: 8 to 9 cups.

SALADS

BROWN RICE SALAD
2 c. Brown Rice, cooked and cooled
2 stalks Celery, chopped
2 Scallions, sliced
1 Carrot, grated
½ c. Mushrooms, sliced, steamed

30 Days To No More PMS
The Cook Book

Combine ingredients and toss.

Dressing:
4 tbsp. Olive Oil
1 tsp. Dill Weed
½ tsp. Pepper
4 tbsp. Rice Vinegar
½ tsp. Salt

Add dressing ingredients and toss with rice mixture.

LEBANESE WHEAT SALAD
1 ½ c. Cracked, bulgur wheat, or buckwheat
3 c. Vegetable stock

Cook grain in vegetable stock or water. Bring stock or water to boil, add grain slowly and keep boiling 5 minutes. Remove from heat, cover pot tightly. Let this mixture stand while preparing other ingredients. Drain (save water for other uses).

Toss with:
½ c. Lentils, cooked
2 Tomatoes, chopped
1 cup Butter lettuce Leaves, chopped
3 tbsp. Olive oil
¼ c. Chives or green onions, chopped fresh
2 tsp. Mint leaves, chopped,
Juice of 2 Lemons
1 tsp. Salt or salt to taste
Pinch garlic powder
Pepper to taste
6-8 Butter lettuce leaves

Fill butter lettuce leaves with wheat mixture and serve. Yield: 6-8 Servings

PEPPER SLAW
8 Peppers, red, green or yellow or form a mixture of all three types of peppers.

30 Days To No More PMS
The Cook Book

Remove skins and seeds and then cut peppers into infinitesimally fine strips. Combine strips with 1 c. thinly sliced cucumber (hot house type preferably) with skin, 1 c. shredded red cabbage. ¼ c. finely chopped onion. Toss with vinaigrette made of 5 tbsp. olive oil and 5 tbsp. rice vinegar and season with ½ tsp. salt, 1 tsp. celery seed, 1 tsp. dry mustard and 1 tsp pepper. Adjust seasoning to taste. Allow mixture to ripen for a few hours before serving, tossing every ½ hour or so.

MUSHROOM-SPROUT DELIGHT
1 lb. Mushrooms, fresh thinly sliced
½ Avocado diced or small wedges
4 tbsp. Lemon juice
¼ c. Scallions, thinly sliced
½ c. Bean sprouts, rinsed in cold water and dried.
4 tbsp. Safflower oil
½ tsp. each Salt and freshly ground pepper
½ c. Alfalfa sprouts

Place sliced mushrooms in a bowl, toss with lemon juice which will prevent them from darkening. Add remaining ingredients except alfalfa sprouts, toss well. Season to taste with salt and pepper. Chill before serving. When ready to serve, sprinkle alfalfa sprouts on top, toss once more, and serve.

SPROUT SALAD
1 lb. Bean or alfalfa sprouts
1 c. Celery, chopped
1 Red apple, unpeeled and chopped
2 Green onions, chopped

Dressing:
4 tbsp. Safflower oil
4 tbsp. Cider or wine vinegar
¼ tsp. Celery seeds

Combine dressing ingredients and toss with vegetables.

30 Days To No More PMS
The Cook Book

WALDORF SALAD
4 medium Red apples, cored, cut in chunks
2 ribs Celery, chopped
½ c. Nuts, chopped
2 tbsp. Raisins
1 tsp. Lemon juice
¼ tsp. each Cinnamon and Nutmeg
Dash of mace (optional)
Small bunch of grapes or several bananas for garnish
Several leaves of lettuce (any type desired)

Mix all ingredients well and chill. Serve on fresh greens, garnished with a small bunch of grapes or chunks of banana right before serving.

This dish can be varied by using different kinds of nuts: pecans, cashews or peanuts. Blue berries can be added for a different direction. ½ c. plain yogurt can be added for creamy texture. Yield: 6-8 servings.

ORIENTAL TUNA SALAD
1 can Tuna, water-packed (7 oz.) drained and flaked
3 tbsp. Water chestnut, chopped finely
2 tbsp. Celery, chopped finely
2 tbsp. Green pepper, chopped finely
2 tbsp. Home Made Oil Mayonnaise
½ tsp. Soy Sauce
Juice of ½ a Lime

Put all the ingredients in a small bowl and toss until thoroughly combined. Yield: ½ cups.

CARIBBEAN SALAD
1 (4 oz. package) Alfalfa sprouts or 3 cups Bean sprouts
2 ripe Mangoes or papayas
1 large or 2 small Avocados
Juice of 1 Lemon
1-2 tbsp. Wine vinegar

30 Days To No More PMS
The Cook Book

½ tsp. Dijon mustard
4 tbsp. Safflower oil
½ tsp. Salt or salt to taste
Freshly ground pepper

Place sprouts in a glass bowl. Peel mangoes or papayas and cut in small chunks. Add to salad bowl. Cut avocados into slices and spread over the sprouts and mangoes or papaya. Sprinkle with lemon juice. In a small bowl, dissolve mustard in vinegar by beating with a fork, beat in oil. Add salt and pepper to taste. Yield: 4 servings.

TUNISIAN SALAD
1 c. ripe Tomatoes, finely chopped
1 c. Green Apple, diced
1 c. Onion, chopped
1 c. Sweet Green Pepper, seeded and finely diced
2 tsp. Hot Green Chili Peppers, seeded and finely chopped
3 tbsp. Wine Vinegar
3 tbsp. Safflower oil
1 tbsp. Dried Mint leaves, pulverized
½ tsp. Salt, pepper to taste

Combine all of the vegetables and the apple in a bowl. Add the vinegar and oil, toss well. Add mint, salt, pepper mix again and serve at room temperature. Yield: 4-6 servings.

MOROCCAN PEPPER SALAD
6 Sweet Peppers
3 tbsp Onions, finely chopped
4 tbsp. Safflower oil
4 tbsp. Lemon juice
½ tsp. Salt and freshly ground
Black Pepper
Cayenne Pepper

Wash peppers and slice off tops. Remove core and seeds; slice thinly and

30 Days To No More PMS
The Cook Book

arrange pepper rings on serving dish. Sprinkle with onions. In bowl, combine oil and lemon juice, season generously with salt, pepper and cayenne. Pour over pepper rings. Yield: 6-8 servings.

DRESSINGS - SAUCES - SPREADS

CELERY SEED DRESSING
4 tbsp. Safflower oil
4 tbsp. Cider or Wine Vinegar
¼ tsp. Celery seeds

NO OIL TOMATO HERB SALAD DRESSING
8 oz. Tomato juice
½ tbsp. Lemon juice
½ tbsp. Vinegar
1 tsp. Worcestershire sauce
1 tsp. Onion juice
2 cloves of Garlic, crushed
2 drops Tabasco
1 tsp. Dry Mustard
1 tsp. Herb mix (rosemary, thyme, basil, chilies, coriander,
 mustard seed, oregano or fennel)

Blend all ingredients together by shaking in a covered container. Yield: 1 ½ cups.

HERB DRESSING
1 tsp. each (dried) Marjoram, dill, basil, oregano, thyme
1 clove Garlic pressed
1 c. Cider Vinegar
1 c. Safflower oil
Dash Cayenne

SALAD DRESSING A LA GOLDEN DOOR
1 c. Tomato puree, fresh or canned
¼ c. Mayonnaise Home Made
1 tbsp. Cider or wine vinegar

30 Days To No More PMS
The Cook Book

1 tbsp. Dry mustard
1 tsp. Dill weed
2 tsp. Lemon juice

Mix in blender.

NO OIL SALAD DRESSING
8 oz. Tomato sauce
2 tbsp. Tarragon Vinegar
1 tsp. Soy Tamari sauce
½ tsp. dried Dill Weed
½ tsp. dried Basil, crushed
1 tbsp. Onion, diced
2 cloves Garlic, minced
1 1" long Chili Pepper ground in mini mill

Put all ingredients in blender and blend until smooth.

HOME MADE OIL MAYONNAISE
1 tsp. Salt
¼ tsp. Mustard
speck of Cayenne
1 tbsp. Lemon juice
1 tbsp. Vinegar
1 Egg, unbeaten
1 c. Safflower oil

Put dry ingredients in mixing bowl. Add lemon juice and vinegar, then mix thoroughly. Add the egg, but do not beat. Add 1/3 of the oil, beat with wheel beater until mixture begins to thicken. Add another 1/3 cup of oil, beat 1 minute, add rest of the oil and then beat 1 minute more. This recipe take about 3 minutes to make. One can substitute tarragon vinegar or wine vinegar for regular vinegar for variations of flavor. If sweetening is necessary you can use one tsp. of frozen unsweetened apple juice concentrate or either Equal or Nutrasweet (aspartame)[*] to taste.

30 Days To No More PMS
The Cook Book

* Aspartame = phenylalanine and is contraindicated for people with phenylketonuria.

HOME MADE CATSUP
5 medium Tomatoes, diced
3 Apples, Red or Green, diced
1 medium Green Pepper, diced
2 medium Onions, diced
½ c. frozen Apple juice concentrate unsweetened or White Grape juice concentrate unsweetened
1 tbsp. Salt
⅛ tsp. Cayenne Pepper
1 c. Vinegar Regular, Tarragon or Wine

Cook the first four ingredients until soft, blend in blender until thick (to your own taste). Add the rest of the ingredients to the above mixture in a sauce pan and boil slowly for 1 hour until thick. Bottle while hot and seal.

THOUSAND ISLAND DRESSING -- HOME MADE
2 tbsp. Green Peppers, minced
2 tbsp. Pimento, minced
1 tsp. Onion juice or Onion, minced
1 tsp. Worcestershire Sauce
1 tbsp. Catsup (Home Made)
½ tsp. Chili powder
1 c. Home Made Oil Mayonnaise
Dash Salt
Dash Paprika

Mix the ingredients except Mayonnaise, add dash of salt and paprika. Blend thoroughly with mayonnaise. For variation add 1 hard cooked egg, chopped. Chili can be increased or decreased to taste. Celery 1-2 tbsp. and or cucumber can be added.

FISH MAIN DISHES

There is little information regarding the magnesium levels in most fish or meats used as main course dishes. What we look for is, 1) those fish or meats known to be low in Calcium content, 2) those fish or meats with the least fat content, and 3) what you make with the fish or meat, i.e., the sauces, gravies and side dishes that accompany the main course food.

As a rule of thumb, do not uses sauces or gravies with sugar, flour or high calcium foods, i.e., dairy. Remember, breading or rolling in flour is to be avoided unless you can use corn flour or other whole grain flours.

There are several fishes that are better than others since their Mg/Ca ratios greater then 1.5.

Mackerel, Atlantic	6.4	Oyster, Pacific, raw	2.7
Swordfish, baked	5.9	Crocker, Atlantic	2.6
Tuna, White, canned	5.0	Haddock	2.5
Sockeye Salmon	4.0	Tuna, Light, canned	2.5
Sea Bass, baked	4.0	Scallops	2.3
Bonito	3.5	Halibut	1.8
Turbo, European	2.9	Red Snapper	1.8
Rockfish, Pacific	2.9	Perch	1.6
Cod	2.8	Crab, Dungeness	1.0

Although the above list is short, there are several types of fish that are specifically low in calcium and/or high enough in magnesium, to be particularly valuable. Oysters may be the single exception, they are quite high in calcium and might be best avoided. The fish listed above are generally commercially available. Halibut and red snapper can often be found fresh in restaurants. If these fish are not available, any fish can be used in moderate 4-6 oz. portions.

EASY FISH
4 Snapper, perch, haddock or halibut, etc. fillets, 4-6 oz each
Tarragon
Dillweed
Onion powder
Whole wheat flour
Freshly ground pepper
Lemon

30 Days To No More PMS
The Cook Book

Preheat broiler. Dip fillets in whole wheat flour, place in shallow backing dish and sprinkle to taste with tarragon, dill weed, onion powder and pepper to taste.

Broil 2 ½ to 3 inches from the heat source about 3-4 minutes (See Table: 6 Fish Tips, regarding cooking times.), baste once with drippings. Turn, baste and sprinkle with additional herbs, if desired. Broil 3 to 4 minutes longer. Serve with lemon wedges. Yield: 4 servings.

POACHED RED SNAPPER
2 Whole red snappers (3 lbs.)
10 c. Water
½ c. Tarragon vinegar
2 Onions, sliced
2 Carrots, sliced
1 Bouquet garni
12 Black peppercorns
Pinch mace
1 Lemon

Have fish cleaned. Bring other ingredients to a boil and simmer 45 minutes in poaching pan (See Poaching Tips Table: 5-1). Poach fish gently 15 minutes per pound, if whole, 15 minutes total cooking time, if fish is in slices. May be served hot or cold, garnished with lemon slices and sprigs of fresh dill. Yield: Depends on number of pieces of fish.

BAKED RED SNAPPER
1 Red snapper, cleaned about 5 lbs.
Freshly ground pepper
½ c. Celery, chopped
3 fresh Jalapeno chilies, seeded and cut in strips.
 You can also substitute green pepper 3/4 c. chopped
1 c. Onion, chopped
1 clove Garlic, pressed
6 lg. Tomatoes, ripe and chopped or 2 c. tomato puree
⅛ tsp. Ground cinnamon
⅛ tsp. Ground cloves

30 Days To No More PMS
The Cook Book

Chili powder or cayenne

Rinse fish well and dry. Saute celery, onions, (green pepper) until vegetables are limp. Add chilies and garlic, if used and 3/4 of the tomatoes; cook a few minutes, stirring occasionally. Pour half the sauce in a greased, shallow backing dish. Lay fish in sauce, fill cavity with sauce. Top with remaining tomatoes, seasoned with chili powder (cayenne), cinnamon and cloves. Bake fish uncovered in preheated 400 degrees F. oven about 45 minutes or until fish is flaky when tested with a fork. Serve fish garnished. Reheat remaining tomato sauce and serve as a side dish with fish and steamed brown rice. Yield: Serves 6.

BAKED FILET OF FISH
1 ½ lb. Fish fillets
½ c. Chicken or vegetable stock
1 tsp. Worcestershire
⅛ c. Rice vinegar
½ tsp. Rosemary
1 lb. fresh Mushroom

Lay fillets in baking pan. Combine other ingredients. Pour over fish, turn fish once. Bake in 350 degrees oven 15-20 minutes. Serve on bed of butter lettuce. Arrange fillets in the center, surround with avocado and papaya slices. Serve with steamed brown rice, wild rice or buckwheat.

This recipe can be varied by using pineapple slices baked over the fish. The fillets can be chosen from the list at the beginning of this chapter.

GRANT AVENUE SAND DABS
3 lbs. dressed Sand Dabs
1 tbsp. grated Ginger
4 Green onions
2 qt. boiling Water
Fringed green onions

Arrange fish in heat-proof platter and sprinkle with ginger. Place 4 whole green onions on top of the fish. Place platter on a trivet or rack inside steamer or large roaster containing boiling water. Cover and steam over boiling water 5 to 10 minutes or until fish flakes easily when tested with a fork. Remove fish from steamer. Discard cooked onions drain any water from platter. Garnish with fringed green onions. Yield: 6 servings.

POACHED SALMON
8 Salmon steaks
3 Black Peppercorns
1 Bay Leaf
2 slices Lemon
2 c. Water
3 sprigs fresh Dill or 1 tsp. dried

Bring water and seasonings to simmer. Place salmon in gently. Cover, simmer for 10-15 minutes Remove from liquid, serve hot or chilled. Yield: 8 serving.

FISH WITH ZUCCHINI
2 Halibut steaks
1 1-inch Ginger, peeled
1 lg. Tomato, sliced
½ c. Onion, minced
2-3 Zucchini, sliced
½ c. Water
Dash of Paprika
Pepper
2 tbsp. Soy sauce

Place fish steaks in a large saucepan or skillet. Top with ginger, tomatoes, onion and zucchini. Add water, paprika, pepper to taste and soy sauce. Garnish with lemon wedges. Yield: 4 servings.

BAKED FISH STUFFING
1 ½ c. Cooked brown or wild rice or whole wheat crumbs
1 ½ tsp. Thyme
1-2 pinches of Pepper to taste
¼ c. Chicken stock

30 Days To No More PMS
The Cook Book

2 tbsp. Celery, chopped
2 tbsp. Onion, chopped

Use to stuff whole fish before baking, or bake fish steaks on stuffing.

CITRUS BAKED SNAPPER
2 lbs. Red snapper fillets
¼ c. Onion, grated
2 tbsp. Orange juice
2 tbsp. Lemon juice
2 tsp. grated Orange peel
⅛ tsp. Nutmeg
⅛ tsp. Pepper
Lemon slices

Cut fish into six portions. Place in a single layer, skin side down in a 12 x 8 in. baking dish. Combine onions, orange and lemon juices, with orange peel. Pour over fish. Cover and refrigerate 30 min. Sprinkle fish with nutmeg and pepper.

Bake uncovered at 350 degrees for 25-30 minutes or until fish flakes easily when tested with a fork. Garnish with lemon slices. Yield: 6 servings.

BAKED SEA BASS
2 lbs. Sea bass fillets
2 tbsp. Lime juice
1 tsp. Salt
¼ tsp. Pepper
1 c. Onion, chopped
1 Bay leaf, crumbled
1 c. Mushrooms, chopped

Cut into serving size portions. Sprinkle with lime juice, salt and pepper. Spread onion over the bottom of a 13 x 9 in. baking dish. Place fillets in a single layer on onions. Top with bay leaf and mushrooms.

Bake at 350 degrees for 20-25 minutes or until fish flakes easily when tested

30 Days To No More PMS
The Cook Book

with a fork. If desired, remove fish to hot serving platter, reduce or thicken pan juices with whole wheat flour and pour over fish. Yield: 6 servings.

FISH-RICE SALAD
3 c. Brown Rice, cooked, cooled
½ c. Celery, minced
½ c. Green Onion, minced
½-1 c. Tomato, chopped
1-1 ½ tsp. dried Basil or Tarragon
1 ½-2 c. cooked fish, chilled and flaked (leftovers are fine)
2 tbsp. Rice Vinegar
½ tsp. Pepper
½ tsp. Dijon mustard
4 tbsp. Olive oil

Gently toss all ingredients together and serve on butter lettuce. Garnish with tomato wedges.

FISH TIPS

1. **Measure fish at thickest point and cook 10 minutes per inch of thickness.**

2. **Poach in liquid that gently simmers. Rapid boiling will break fish apart. Wrap fish in cheesecloth to hold together for easy removal, if desired.**

3. **To cook wrapped fish - lay on parchment paper first, then on a larger piece of foil. Season, fold in packet, bake at 450 degrees.**

4. **If the type of fish is named in the recipe use that fish or substitute whatever fresh fish is available at your market.**

5. **Fresh fish is preferable to frozen. Buy your fish on the way home, and use it that day. Always pick fish closest to the ice.**

6. **If you do use frozen fish, be sure it's completely frozen and keep it so till ready to cook (5 degrees or colder).**

7. **To cook frozen fish whole or in 1 lb. block of fillets. Cook 20-24 minutes per inch of thickness. Do not defrost first but let it stand at room temperature 15 minutes.**

Table 8

30 Days To No More PMS
The Cook Book

SAUCE FOR BROILED FISH

2 tbsp. Lemon juice

2 tsp. Mustard

2 tsp. Horseradish

¼ tsp. Pepper

Paprika

Place fish filets in broiler and brush on both sides. Broil fish until just flaky (turns white or no longer stiff) serve with brown rice, baked potato or grain dish.

POACHING AND STEAMING FISH

Seasoning for stocks:

Aromatic - Spices	Herbs	Aromatic-Vegetables
capers	thyme	carrot
chili whole	bay leaf	celery
cloves whole	dill	garlic
mace	fennel	green pepper
mixed pickling spices	basil	onion
whole pepper		pimento
vinegar		tomato
curry powder		dried mushrooms
dried horseradish		lemon
ginger		
nutmeg		
peppercorns		
all spice berries		
bay leaf		

SAMPLE POACHING LIQUID
1 qt. Water
1 Onion, sliced
6 Black peppercorns
2 Allspice berries
3 tbsp. Lemon juice
1 Bay leaf
1 tsp. Salt

Table 9

30 Days To No More PMS
The Cook Book

MEAT MAIN DISHES

Many women are accustomed to having meat several times a day. Meats are high in calories, fat and protein. We have already discussed reasons for reducing large amounts of protein and fat during the critical period of the PMS cycle. You may also want to reduce meats because of their enormous number of calories and the weight they can put on you. We strongly suggest that you stay away from pork and pork products, as they tend to be highly salted, preserved with nitrites and very fatty. To this end we will not give any pork recipes.

In any case if you eat meats use only the leanest cuts available, trim all visible excess fat, and where possible drain or remove fat, during and after cooking. Limit portion sizes to no more than 4 to 6 ounces, if possible. All meat dishes (including leftovers) can be frozen, for quick dinners at another time. Use freezer bags or a Seal-A-Meal device to maintain freshness.

BEEF MAIN DISHES

HAMBURGER SAUTE'
1 lb. Hamburger, extra lean
1 medium Onion, sliced
1 c. Mushrooms, sliced or diced
½ tsp. Thyme
½ tsp. Oregano
½ tsp. Salt
¼ tsp. Black Pepper
½ tsp. Garlic Powder
½ tsp. Curry Powder *Optional*

Preheat a heavy skillet slowly, using either 1-2 tbsp. of margarine or safflower oil (or Pam, if on a fat restricted diet) saute' onions, mushrooms, set aside. Mix spices in hamburger meat and form into patties and cook until done to your taste. Top with onions and mushroom mixture. *For variety use curry along with other spices. Yield: 4 servings.

BEEF BARLEY STEW
2 lbs. Chuck beef, stewing cut 1"cubes
¼ c. Safflower Oil
½ c. Barley, uncooked, raw

30 Days To No More PMS
The Cook Book

3/4 c. Onion, diced
1 c. medium Mushrooms, fresh
1 tsp. Salt
¼ tsp. Black Pepper
½ tsp. Marjoram Leaves
⅛ tsp. Tarragon Leaves
1 Bay leaf
1 tbsp. Vegit or any Low sodium vegetable seasoning
2 Carrots
4 medium Potatoes
2 small Onions
2 c. Beef Stock or water

Brown meat in safflower oil. Add meat, seasonings and stock or water. Add barley cover and simmer 1 ½ hours or until meat is almost tender. Scrub carrots well and cut into 1-inch pieces. Scrub potatoes and cut into quarters. Peel onions and cut into quarters. Add vegetables to stew and continue cooking 30 minutes or until vegetables are tender. (If you wish to thicken the broth, make a thin paste by mixing together ¼ c. whole wheat or corn flour with an equal amount of water; stir into the stew and cook, stirring occasionally, until thickened.) Chicken and chicken stock can be substituted in this recipe instead of beef and beef stock. Yield: 4-6 servings.

ROLLED RIB ROAST ROYALE
1 4 to 5 lb. Rolled rib roast or rib eye roast
3 tsp. Bon Appetite or Italian Herb Mix
⅛ tsp. Garlic powder
¼ tsp. Onion salt
½ tsp. Black pepper
4-6 tbsp. Dijon mustard
1 tbsp. Margarine, melted

Combine seasonings, Dijon mustard, margarine and rub thoroughly into meat. Place on rack in pan. Insert a meat thermometer into the center of the thickest part. Roast in 325 degrees F. oven 2 hours for rare, or until meat thermometer registers desired degree of doneness. Baste meat with juices while roasting. Serve on a platter garnished with parsley and crab apples. Yield: 8 to 10.

30 Days To No More PMS
The Cook Book

MEAT LOAF WITH MUSHROOMS
1 lb Beef, ground
1 lb Veal, ground (or ½ lb. veal and ½ lb. turkey)
2 Eggs, beaten
2 tbsp. Onions, minced
2 tsp. Horseradish
2 tsp. Garlic salt
½ tsp. dry Mustard
1 tsp. Season-All
½ c. Whole wheat bread crumbs, soft
½ c. Celery, chopped
1 c. Mushrooms, sliced
¼ c. Stock (chicken or beef)
½ c. Green pepper, chopped

Mix together all the ingredients until blended, being careful not to over mix. Shape into loaf in shallow baking pan, or put in loaf pan. Bake in 375 degrees F. oven 1 ½ hours. For variety you can add ½ to 1 c. cashews. Turkey can be entirely substituted for beef or veal.

BEEF TAMALE PIE
1 lb. Beef, ground
½ tsp. Garlic salt
½ tsp. Chili powder
½ c. Onions, chopped
Tamale Pie Basic recipe from Vegetable Main Dish section.

Saute' ground meat, onions, garlic salt, and chili powder. Using the basic recipe for tamale pie layer cooked ground beef into it as you make it. Yield: Serves 6.

VEAL MAIN DISHES

VEAL CUTLET SUPERIOR
2 Veal cutlets
2 Eggs, beaten
½ c. Whole wheat flour

30 Days To No More PMS
The Cook Book

Salt and pepper
¼ tsp. Curry powder
1 tbsp. Margarine

Mix ingredients together and bread cutlets. Saute' in small amount of margarine. Vary by adding to the saute' ½ lb. Mushrooms, sliced or 1 tbsp. Lemon juice or both. Yield: Serves 2.

VEAL STEW MENAGERIE
1 ½ lb. Veal shank
3 tbsp. Margarine
8 small Onions, peeled
8 small Potatoes, whole scrubbed
2 Carrots, cut wide chunks
1 tbsp. Whole wheat flour
1 ½ c. Consomme' or stock

Saute' diced veal cut into 1 ½ inch cubes in margarine. Add onions. Remove meat and onions from pan. Pour off all but 1 tbsp. of fat. Stir in flour until smooth. Add and stir consomme'. Add meat, onions, potatoes and carrots. You can add 2 stalks of celery diced if you desire. Simmer covered until very tender, 1 ½ to 2 hours. Season and serve. Yield: Serves 4.

LAMB MAIN DISHES

CURRY OF LAMB WITH BROWN RICE
2 lbs. Lamb shoulder, cubed
3 tbsp. Safflower oil
4 tbsp. Onion, fresh, chopped
2 tsp. Salt
¼ tsp. Mustard, dry
4 tbsp. Curry powder
1 c. Stock (vegetable, beef or chicken)
2 tbsp. Lemon juice
1 tart Apple, cored and diced
2 tbsp. fresh Coconut, grated

30 Days To No More PMS
The Cook Book

2 tbsp. chopped dry roasted Peanuts or 2 tbsp. raw cashews
2 tbsp. Seedless raisins or currants ash of nutmeg

Remove gristle and fat from the meat. Cut into 1" cubes. Brown meat in oil. Add onions to skillet; saute ingredients for a few minutes but do not brown. Add remaining ingredients; mix well. (For a milder curry add less curry powder, for hot curry, increase the amount of curry powder.) Cover and simmer for 45 minutes or until tender. Stir frequently. Serve over brown rice.
Make: 1 c. brown rice, 2 c. water cook for 1 hour. Chicken, beef, shrimp, or 2 medium eggplants may be substituted for lamb in this dish. Yield: 4 servings.

LAMB SHANK DIVINE
4 Lamb shanks
2 tbsp. Whole wheat flour
1 tsp. Sage leaves, crumbled
½ tsp. Oregano leaves
½ tsp. Celery salt
1 ½ tsp. Season-All
½ tsp. Black pepper
½ c. Onions, minced
½ tsp. Garlic salt
2 tbsp. Lemon juice
1 8 oz. Tomato sauce
½ c. Water
2 tbsp. Margarine or Safflower oil

Roll lamb shanks in whole wheat flour seasoned with Season-All (you can use any seasoning product such as Italian Herbs, Spike, Vegit, etc. per your tastes and what you have available) and pepper. Brown in hot oil or margarine. Combine remaining ingredients and pour over the meat. Cover and simmer gently for 1 ½ hours or until tender. Excellent with wild rice or brown rice. Yield: Serves 4.

RAGOUT OF LAMB ROSEMARY
2 lbs. Lamb, lean, cubed
2 tbsp. Whole wheat flour
2 c. Beef stock

30 Days To No More PMS
The Cook Book

1 tbsp. Safflower oil
¼ tsp. Rosemary leaves
1 Bay leaf
3 Potatoes
3 Carrots
½ tsp. Mint flakes
¼ tsp. Garlic, minced
¼ c. Onions, chopped
1 tsp. Celery salt
1 tsp. Season-All
2 tbsp. Margarine

Slowly brown lamb on all sides in oil. Add seasoning and beef stock, gently simmer 1 ½ hours or until lamb is almost tender. Scrub potatoes and carrots. Cut potatoes into quarters and carrots into 2-inch pieces, add to stew. Simmer 40 minutes or until vegetables are tender. In a separate pan, melt margarine, add flour and cook until flour is brown, stirring constantly. Stir into stew and cook a few minutes longer to thicken. Serve with brown rice or over millet. Yield: Serves 4 to 6.

POULTRY MAIN DISHES

CHICKEN MAIN DISHES

The PMS woman is best advised to stay away from heavy red meats such as beef, lamb, veal or pork. She would do best with fish and fowl: chicken, turkey, and duck on occasion.

STUFFED CHICKEN LEGS
8 Fresh Chicken Legs
4 c. Brown Rice with Mushrooms (See Grain Side Dishes)
¼ c. Safflower oil
½ c. Fresh Bean Sprouts
¼ c. Water Chestnuts, chopped
4 tbsp Soy Sauce
2 Fresh Garlic Cloves
¼ tsp. Ginger

30 Days To No More PMS
The Cook Book

Dash of Nutmeg
¼ tsp. dry Mustard
1 ½ tsp. Salt
½ c. Water or chicken stock *optional*
Dash of Paprika

Wash chicken legs, leave skin on and dry. Combine brown rice with mushrooms, safflower oil, water chestnuts and bean sprouts. Stir in soy sauce, and spices. Add salt and pepper to taste. Fill each chicken leg with approx ½ cup of brown rice mixture. Place in a casserole dish (pour water or chicken stock over the top of the stuffed legs if desired more moist) and bake in oven covered for 45 minutes at 350 degrees F. Uncover and bake for an additional 10 minutes. Turn each piece over sprinkle with a little paprika and continue to bake for 10 more minutes or until golden brown. (If you prefer you may broil the chicken legs for 5 minutes on each side instead). Option: Use the meaty part of the chicken wings instead (drummette). Yield: 4 servings.

HAWAIIAN CHICKEN NANI
8 Chicken thighs or 4 Chicken half breasts or wings (drummettes)
1 lb. Mushrooms, fresh, medium size
1 Sweet Bell Pepper, medium chopped (remove the seeds)
1 small Onion, sliced into strips
3 Snap beans, fresh, cleaned and cut into 1" segments
3 tbsp. Soy sauce
¼ tsp. Ginger

Cut meat off of the thighs, leaving a small amount of meat just around the bone. Place meat, bones, and onion into a pot and lightly brown. (Add 1-2 tbsp. water if necessary). Add mushrooms, bell pepper, snap beans, water chestnuts, soy sauce and ginger. Cook for just a few minutes to slightly steam the vegetables. For variety add ¼ cup pineapple, crushed. Serve immediately over a bed of rice. The rice can be chosen from one of the dishes from this book. Yield : 4 servings.

CHICKEN KEBOBS
2 lbs. Chicken breast meat cut into 2 inch cubes
2 tsp. Vegit or other low sodium vegetable seasoning

30 Days To No More PMS
The Cook Book

½ tsp. Black pepper, coarsely ground
½ tsp. Oregano Leaves
4 Onions, small, skinned
½ lb. Mushrooms, large fresh
⅛ Thyme Leaves
2 tbsp. Lemon juice
¼ c. Safflower Oil
4 Cherry Tomatoes
1 Sweet Bell Pepper, large
2 tbsp. melted Margarine or Safflower Oil

Cut meat into 2-inch cubes. Combine seasonings, lemon juice and ¼ c. oil; pour over meat. Cover and marinate in refrigerator 1 hour, turning meat several times. Cut green pepper into 1-inch squares and remove outer skin of onions. Brush vegetables with melted margarine or oil. Thread meat, tomatoes, green pepper, mushrooms and onions onto skewers alternating meat with vegetables. Barbecue or broil 4 inches from heat for 8 minutes, turn and continue broiling 6 minutes longer or until meat is nicely browned. Brush with marinade several times while cooking. Serve with brown and wild rice recipe. Yield: 4 servings.

ARROZ CON POLLO
1 3-lb. Chicken
1 tbsp. Pimento, chopped
1 tbsp. Season-All or Vegit
⅛ tsp. Garlic, minced
¼ tsp. Black pepper, coarsely ground
1 Bay leaf
⅛ tsp. Saffron, crushed
⅛ tsp. Cayenne or Red pepper
¼ c. Whole wheat flour
½ c. Safflower oil
1 medium Green pepper
2-3 Tomatoes
1 c. Mushrooms, sliced
1 c. Green peas
2 c. Brown rice
5 c. Chicken stock

30 Days To No More PMS
The Cook Book

Cut chicken in pieces, dredge with mixture of Season-All or Vegit, pepper and whole wheat flour. Brown in hot Safflower oil in a skillet. Place browned chicken in a 4-quart casserole. Chop green pepper and saute' with onions in remaining hot oil until onions are lightly browned. Cut tomatoes into pieces. Add tomatoes, mushrooms, chicken stock, rice, pimento, and seasonings. Mix thoroughly and pour over chicken. Cover and bake 375 degrees F. oven 40 minutes. Add peas and continue baking, covered, 15 to 20 minutes longer. Serve hot. Yield: Serves 6.

BROILED CHICKEN
2 2-lb. Chicken, broilers cut in half lengthwise
½ c. Margarine, melted
1 tsp. Salt (Garlic or Celery salt is acceptable)
1 tbsp. Season-All
½ tsp. Onion powder

Break up or cut chicken into pieces so that the chicken will lay flat while broiling. Put, skin side down, on broiling rack. Combine remaining ingredients and brush over the chicken. Broil 5 to 7 inches from heat 15 minutes. Turn chicken and brush with seasoned margarine, 15 minutes longer. Continue turning and basting chicken every 15 minutes until drumstick is tender and shows pink when cut. Total cooking time is about 45 minutes.

VARIATIONS ON BROILED CHICKEN:

HERB BROILED CHICKEN
Substitute 2 tsp. Italian Herb Seasoning, 2 tsp. Garlic salt, 1 tbsp. Bon Appetite and ½ tsp. Paprika for the above seasonings.

CHILI BROILED CHICKEN
Substitute 2 tsp. salt, 1 tbsp. Chili powder for above seasonings.

CORIANDER BROILED CHICKEN
Substitute 2 tsp. crushed coriander seeds and add to seasonings above.

CURRY BROILED CHICKEN
Substitute 2 tsp. Indian curry into margarine mixture.

30 Days To No More PMS
The Cook Book

DIJON BROILED CHICKEN

Substitute Dijon mustard into margarine mixture.

POLYNESIAN CHICKEN

1 3-lb. Chicken, cut into pieces
Soy sauce
White distilled Vinegar
1 medium Lime, cut and squeezed
3 stalks Green onions, chopped
1 tbsp. Garlic powder

Mix Soy sauce and white distilled vinegar in equal parts in sufficient amounts to cover all the chicken parts. Add green onions, garlic powder, lime both juice and slices. Marinate chicken from 1 hour to overnight according to your taste. Save this marinade in sealed jar in refrigerator as it can be used again. This can be served with brown rice, baked potato, corn on the cob, or a cooked grain. Yield: Serves 4. Great for summer BBQ.

OVEN FRIED CHICKEN

1 3 lb. Chicken, pieces
1 tsp. Vegit
½ c. Margarine, melted
⅛ tsp. Onion powder
1 tsp. Salt
½ tsp. Dill Weed
¼ tsp. Black pepper
¼ tsp. Paprika
Whole wheat flour

Clean and dry chicken. Mix margarine, salt. Vegit. onion powder, dill weed and paprika into a paste like consistency. Dredge chicken in whole wheat flour and place skin side down, in shallow pan. Spoon margarine mixture over chicken. Cook in 425 degrees F. oven 30 minutes. Turn chicken and spoon on margarine mixture and then cook 15 minutes more or until tender and brown. Yield: Serves 3 to 4.

30 Days To No More PMS
The Cook Book

TURKEY MAIN DISHES

ROAST TURKEY
1 Turkey (weight to fit your family's needs) or turkey parts
¼ c. Melted margarine
1 tbsp. Curry powder
2-3 tbsp. Dijon mustard
1 tbsp. Italian Herb mixture
1 tbsp Worcestershire sauce or A-1 sauce

Mix the ingredients together and brush on to turkey. Place the turkey breast down in oven pan, cover with tin foil. Preheat oven to 450 degrees F. Reduce immediately to 350 degrees F., or 325 degrees F. for large birds. Uncover for the last 1 ½ hours. For turkey less than 6 lbs. 20 to 25 minutes per pound. For birds greater than 6 to 16 lbs. allow 15 to 20 minutes per pound. For turkeys greater than 16 lbs. allow 13 to 15 minutes per pound. Add 5 minutes per pound if cooked with stuffing.

MUSHROOM-RICE STUFFING

½ c. Margarine	½ tsp. Salt
3 c. Brown rice, cooked	⅛ tsp. Black pepper
3 tbsp. Onions, chopped	⅛ tsp. Thyme, ground
2 c. Celery, diced	1 tsp. Chicken seasoned stock base
½ tsp. Marjoram	2/3 c. Pecans, chopped
1 c. Mushrooms, sliced	

Melt the margarine in a large skillet, add remaining ingredients; except the pecans. Saute', stirring until lightly browned. Remove from the heat and add pecans, toss gently. Use as a side dish or stuff in turkey, chicken or fish. Bake in a casserole in 325 degrees F. oven 30 minutes. Yield: 6 cups.

WILD RICE STUFFING

1 c. Wild rice, cooked	¼ tsp. Black pepper
1 tsp. Season-All or Vegit	1 ½ tsp. Chicken seasoned stock base
1 c. Celery, chopped	¼ tsp. Thyme leaves
¼ c. Onions, chopped	½ tsp. Salt

30 Days To No More PMS
The Cook Book

½ c. Margarine, melted
1 c. Mushrooms, sliced
¼ tsp. Oregano leaves
½ tsp. Marjoram leaves
2 tbsp. Water

Cook wild rice as directed on package, adding seasoned stock base to the water. Saute' celery and onions in the margarine. Then combine all ingredients and mix well. Yield: 6 cups, enough to stuff a 10 lb. bird.

TURKEY STEW DELIGHT
5 lbs. Turkey pieces, disjointed or cubed
¼ c. Margarine or Safflower oil
½ c. Onions, chopped
1 ½ c. Tomatoes, quartered
3 c. Lima Beans, fresh is better then frozen but frozen can be used
⅛ tsp. Cayenne
3 c. Corn, cut from the cob
2 tsp. Worcestershire sauce

This recipe can be made with chicken, chicken and turkey or fish in equal parts. Dice the turkey meat into cubes about 1" in size. Saute' slowly in margarine or oil until light brown. Remove meat from the pan and brown onions. Place the meat in a large stewing pan, pour onions over the meat, add tomatoes, lima beans, cayenne, here you can add in the other variations such as chili peppers (amount depends on how hot you would like the stew) or mustard. Add corn, cover and simmer the mixture until meat is tender. Season to taste with salt and freshly ground pepper. Add Worcestershire sauce. If you desire, you can add 1 c. toasted whole wheat bread crumbs prior to serving. Yield: Serves 8.

ROAST TURKEY BREAST
1 Turkey breast, 3 ½ to 7 lbs.
¼ c. Margarine
½ tsp. Curry
⅛ tsp. Thyme
⅛ tsp. Basil
⅛ tsp. Marjoram

Mix melted margarine and curry with herbs, brush mixture on turkey. Place the

30 Days To No More PMS
The Cook Book

breast in a shallow pan. Preheat oven to 450 degrees F. Reduce the heat to 325 degrees F. and roast uncovered, basting frequently. Allow about 20 minutes per pound. Serve with brown rice, millet, baked potato or any grain dish of your choice. Yield: Allow 1/3 lb. per serving.

DUCK MAIN DISHES

ROAST DUCK
1 Duckling, 4 to 5 lbs.
2 tbsp. Margarine
2 tbsp. Dijon mustard

Mix margarine and Dijon mustard together and brush on the duckling. Preheat oven to 450 degrees F. Place the duckling on a rack in a roasting pan. For crisper skin pierce the skin several times for fat to drain. You may stuff the bird with using a recipe from this book (see turkey stuffing) or roast unstuffed. Put the bird, uncovered into the oven and reduce the heat to 350 degrees F. Cook until tender, allowing about 20 minutes per pound for the unstuffed bird and longer for the stuffed bird. For variation of this recipe you can substitute the following 1) Curry powder, 1 tbsp. 2) Italian herb mixture 3) Crushed pineapple in natural juice 4) Garlic and paprika instead of Dijon mustard or with Dijon mustard. Yield: When quartered 4 servings per duckling. Note: Save the duck broth, see below.

DUCK PILAF
1 Roasted Duckling, made as above
4 c. Water or chicken stock
1 Onion, chopped
Celery leaves
Salt and Paprika
1 c. left over Duck liquor (pour off fat, if possible)
2 tbsp. Margarine
2/3 c. Brown or Wild rice
3/4 c. Celery, chopped finely
1 tsp. Onion, grated

Remove the meat from the duck, this should yield about 2 cups of meat. Break up the carcass. Mix together meat (meat can be wrapped in cheese cloth to facilitate later separation), carcass and water or chicken stock, chopped onions and celery leaves. Simmer this stock covered for one hour. Strain. Bring to boiling point. Cook the rice until tender, about ½ hour. Strain it. Reserve the liquor. Melt the margarine. Saute' celery and grated onion until browned slightly. Add duck meat, rice and duck liquor. Mix all well with fork. Season to taste with salt and paprika. As a variation cover the duck with whole pitted nectarines roasted on top of the duck. Yield: Serves 4.

SANDWICHES

Everyone loves sandwiches whether it is for lunch, dinner or even for a picnic. The PMS woman is probably no exception however, she will have some special considerations. We have talked about the basic fundamental considerations sugar, calcium, food additives etc. When choosing and making sandwiches the PMS woman must keep these in mind.

The bread (women with severe PMS might consider purchasing a bread maker so that they can make their own healthy bread) chosen, as well as any bread eaten with meals, must be picked carefully. *Read the label* look for bleached flour content, for honey, corn syrup, corn sweetener, molasses, sugar in any form; also fat or lard, etc. Watch for additives, such as coloring or preservatives. Breads with a high content of these substances should generally be avoided.

The bread you chose would be best, if it has unbleached flour, whole grains, sprouted grains, little or no sugar or sugar-like products and is as free of additives and fat, as is possible.

After you have picked or baked your bread, what goes into it, is extremely important. This applies the main ingredients or spreads that you use on the breads. You must be careful of sandwich spreads with mayonnaise, as they too are high in dairy (calcium), sugar and fats. Commercial ketchup's are generally high in sugar. *Read labels!* It is most important that you think ahead and become creative. When you buy commercially made sandwiches, it is likely that they will be high in calcium, sugar and additives. So be careful!

See the section on bread for further details about bread. Remember, pita and corn tortillas can also be used to make sandwiches.

30 Days To No More PMS
The Cook Book

SALAD IN A SANDWICH
Heat Pita or Bible bread. When heated, open bread and fill with the following; Cooked pinto or red beans, chili, small amounts of sprouts, onions, tomatoes with a dash of Picante sauce (you can either make this on your own or buy it at the market) add avocado or sliced zucchini along with grated carrots. For a taste treat vary contents add pecans, walnuts or cashews.

TUNA DELIGHT
1 small can Tuna, water packed
½ c. Pineapple, chopped
2 tsp. Almond (cashews, walnuts, pecans or peanuts can be substituted)
2 tbsp. Onion, chopped
Pinch of Dill
2 tbsp. Home Made Oil Mayonnaise

Drain the tuna of most of its water. Combine with pineapple, nuts, onions, dill, and homemade mayonnaise. Mix well and fill pita.

PEANUT BUTTER AND JELLY
Rice cake or whole wheat bread
Pure peanut butter (cashew or almond butter)
Westbrae Natural unsweetened fruit spreads (raspberry, blackberry, strawberry)
Fresh crushed berries or fruit can also be used.
Sliced banana can be marvelous.

Serve open or closed with whole wheat bread.

AVOCADO DELIGHT
1-2 slices Whole wheat bread
1 small Avocado, sliced
Home Made Oil Mayonnaise
1-2 Leaf butter or iceberg lettuce

Can be served as open or closed sandwich.

AVOCADO DELICIOUS
1-2 slices Whole wheat bread

30 Days To No More PMS
The Cook Book

1 small Avocado
2 tbsp. Cashews
1 small Banana, sliced

Mash avocado and cashews separately and then mix together spread mixture avocado-cashews on the bread layer banana slices over mix eat as either open face or as regular sandwich add a few drops lemon juice to avocado to keep from discoloring if not eaten immediately.

TURKEY DELIGHT
1-2 slices Whole wheat bread
Several slices white meat turkey (3 oz.)
Home Made Oil Mayonnaise
1 small Avocado, sliced
1-2 leaf Butter lettuce

Can be served as open or closed sandwich. Chicken or duck slices may also be used.

JICAMA SANDWICH
1 Jicama root, peeled and sliced
Several slices tomato
Darkest leaves of lettuce
Several slices cucumber
2 slices Avocado, dipped in lemon juice

Place tomato and lettuce on one piece of jicama. Top with stack with cucumber and another piece of jicama, avocado slices and finish with a third slice of jicama.
Yield: Serves 1.

GRAINS, BEANS AND VEGETABLES DISHES

GRAIN AND BEAN DISHES

It is a good rule of thumb to suggest that during the PMS time of the month, every meal should include either a grain or vegetable dish or both. This is not only to round the meal off and add

30 Days To No More PMS
The Cook Book

to the completeness of the meal, but this is also vitally important to the well-being of the PMS women. Grains and vegetables can generally be a great source of *magnesium* and of *complex carbohydrates*. Grains and vegetables are both necessary in order to provide adequate amounts of *FIBER* to the diet. They are both generally "live" foods and provide other essential vitamins and minerals necessary for good health. They are also usually low in cholesterol, as they have no animal fat component unless mixed with butter or animal fats.

Information about grains is found in two sections of this book. In this section we discuss their use as part of the main meal. You can also find information on how to use grains within breads in Section II, Chapter 1. Whether grains are used as a main dish or a side dish or as a bread they have the same values for PMS women and in fact can always be substituted for the other as long as the grain dish or bread is entirely whole grain and without refined flour and without sugar in any of its many forms.

The grain dish may also be served as a breakfast meal. Virtually all of the dishes presented within this work can be eaten either hot or cold as a main dish, side dish or breakfast meal. The PMS woman should immediately begin to learn to eat grains as often as she can, as they are filling and an excellent source of magnesium, low in calories, and therefore leaves a smaller space for other less valuable foods.

Beans or Legumes are also an excellent source of protein and of complex carbohydrates. They often vary as a source of magnesium and may be slightly higher in calcium. This is all right as they are a good overall source of nutrition. To get full appreciation of how to use beans as part of a well-balanced nutritional program, I would suggest *DIET FOR A SMALL PLANET* by Frances Moore Lappe, Ballantine/Cookbook. This book is an excellent source book for ways to combine beans and grains to make complete proteins.

Last but not least, vegetables are often over looked by PMS women. Those women who do enjoy vegetables often tend to gravitate to vegetables which can be higher in calcium such as broccoli, lettuce, greens, cabbage, celery, squash, etc. While these are excellent foods and can be delightful with almost any main dish, they do present certain problems during the PMS period of the month.

Learning to use the list in Appendixes 2 and 3 can be extremely helpful in choosing good tasting yet PMS fighting vegetables which will support eliminating PMS. Again we refer you to *Diet For A Small Planet* for more information and additional recipes for healthful vegetables. Use Appendix 2 and 3 to pick those vegetables which will help you eliminate your PMS

30 Days To No More PMS
The Cook Book

symptoms.

MILLET PILAF
1 c. Millet
3 c. Vegetable stock or water
1 diced Carrot
1 diced Green Pepper
2 Green Onions, chopped
½ c. diced Mushrooms
1 Bay Leaf
½ tsp. Nutmeg

stock to a boil, add millet and other ingredients. Cook until done, approximately 45 minutes. Yield: 6-7 servings.

COOKED GRANOLA
½ c. Rolled Oats
½ c. Millet
½ c. Buckwheat

This dish can be cook overnight by adding just enough water to cover the grain then follow the instructions given in either Table: 10 or 11. In the morning bring to a boil, cook 5-10 minutes till millet and buckwheat are tender. Serve with some chopped cashews or peanuts and raisins, if your specific needs allow. Add fresh banana, coconut meat (dried or fresh, or nectarines in season. A small serving of non-fat or low-fat milk. If you wish further fortification add several tablespoons of wheat germ as desired.

CHILI EXTRODINAIRE
1 c. Red Beans
1 Green Pepper, diced
2 stalks Celery, diced
1 lbs. Mushrooms, diced
1 Onion, diced
1-2 cloves Garlic, crushed or pressed
Chili powder to taste
Cumin to taste

30 Days To No More PMS
The Cook Book

1 small can Tomato paste
4-6 med. Tomatoes, diced

Soak red beans overnight in water to which garlic and onions have been added. Cook until tender in the morning. In separate sauce pan add and cook until tender: tomatoes, green pepper, celery and mushrooms. Combine beans and vegetables and stir in can of tomato paste. Add cumin and chili powder to desired taste.

This dish can be varied by adding white beans, brown beans, turkey sausage, ground or pieces of chicken, turkey, or beef.

CUBAN BLACK BEANS AND RICE
2 Qts. Water
1 lb. Black Beans
1 Onion, sliced
1 Green Pepper, sliced
1 clove Garlic, crushed
1 tsp. Oregano
1 Bay Leaf
2 tbsp. Cider Vinegar
½ tsp Pepper

Cook all ingredients 3 hrs. or until beans are tender. Cook brown rice (see Table 10) Serve over 1 cup brown rice. Garnish with tomato wedges, chopped green onions.

RICE AND SPROUTED RYE
1 c. Brown Rice
1 c. Chicken stock or water
1 medium Onion chopped
1 c. Mushrooms chopped
1 c. Sprouted Rye

Soak rice in liquid 4-5 hours. Add chopped onions and cook 30 minutes or until tender. Fold in sprouted rye and parsley and heat to serving temperature but don't cook. Yield: 6 Servings.

30 Days To No More PMS
The Cook Book

COOKING GRAINS AND BEANS

GRAIN (1 cup dry measure)	WATER	COOKING TIME	YIELD
Barley (whole)	3 cups	1 hour 15 min.	3 ½ cups
Brown Rice	2 cups	1 hour	3 cups
Buckwheat (kasha)	2 cups	15 minutes	2 ½ cups
Bulgur wheat	2 cups	15-20 minutes	2 ½ cups
Cracked wheat	2 cups	25 minutes	2 ⅓ cups
Millet	3 cups	45 minutes	3 ½ cups
Coarse cornmeal (polenta)	4 cups	25 minutes	3 cups
Wild Rice	3 cups	1 hour or more	4 cups
Whole Wheat Berries	3 cups	2 hours	2 ⅔ cups
Black Beans	3 cups	1 hour	2 cups
Black-eyed Peas	3 cups	1 hour	2 cups
Garbanzos (Chickpeas)	4 cups	3 hours	2 cups
Great Northern Beans	3 ½ cups	2 hours	2 cups
Kidney Beans	3 cups	1 1/2 hours	2 cups
Lentils and Split Peas	3 cups	1 hour	2 ¼ cups
Lima Beans	2 cups	1 1/2 hours	1 ¼ cups
Baby Lima Beans	2 cups	1 1/2 hours	1 ¾ cups
Pinto Beans	3 cups	2 ½ hours	2 cups
Red Beans	3 cups	3 hours	2 cups
Small White Beans (Navy)	3 cups	1 1/2 hours	2 cups

Table 10

COOKING GRAINS OVERNIGHT METHOD

This method of cooking works especially well with grains that take a long time.... whole wheat berries, whole rye and whole oats, etc. The night before, place grains and cold water (see Table 10 for amounts) in a sauce pan. Bring to a boil, turn down to a simmer, simmer covered for 10 minutes. Turn off fire, leave pan tightly covered overnight. In the morning you will have cooked whole grain. Top with small amount skim or low fat milk (watch the amount so that it does not increase you PMS symptoms), a sliced banana or other fresh fruit, a sprinkle of nutmeg or allspice and breakfast is ready. This then provides a whole grain nutritious treat. A perfect food for the PMS woman.

    This dish can be reheated and used as the grain portion for other meals. It can be frozen and stored for later use although the fresher the better.

    Any of the grains can be used either as a breakfast cereal, hot or cold, or as an accompanying dish with dinner vegetables, meat or fish.

Table 11

30 Days To No More PMS
The Cook Book

30 Days To No More PMS
The Cook Book

30 Days To No More PMS
The Cook Book

30 Days To No More PMS
The Cook Book

BROWN RICE AND PINE NUTS

1 c. Brown Rice

½ c. Bulgur Wheat

½ c. Pine Nuts

1 lg. Onion, chopped

6 tbsp. Chives or Scallions, minced

¼ tsp. Pepper

5 c. boiling homemade Chicken or vegetable broth.

Place in a casserole dish and then bake at 375 degrees for 1 hour. Yield: 8-10 Servings

BARLEY CASSEROLE

2 Onions, chopped

3/4 c. fresh Mushrooms, chopped

1 ½ c. Barley

2 c. Chicken, beef or vegetable broth

½ tsp. Salt

⅛ tsp. Cayenne Pepper

Place in a casserole dish and then bake at 350 degrees for 50 minutes. Yield: 4-6

30 Days To No More PMS
The Cook Book

Servings.

FRIED RICE

1 cup Brown Rice	2 Eggs
¼ cup raw Cashews	½ tsp. Salt
1 oz. cooked Chicken	2 ½ tbsp Peanut Oil
3 Scallions	1 ¼ tbsp. Soy Sauce.

Prepare rice as instructed in Table 10. Cool, cover and place in the refrigerator or in a cool place overnight. Split and cut the cashews in half; toast them lightly by placing them in the grill pan under a very hot grill for a few minutes, until golden. Stir occasionally and watch that they do not burn. Cut the chicken into long thin strips and chop the scallions into ¼ inch lengths. Beat the eggs and salt together well. Heat the oil in a large frying pan. Add the egg and fry until it is half cooked. Add the rice (make sure that there are no lumps) and coat the grains in egg, stirring quickly. Keep stirring and turning the rice over and over. Add the chicken and onions and sprinkle in the soy sauce. Fry for 3-4 minutes, stirring constantly. Serve in a heated serving dish sprinkled with the cashews. Yield: 4-6 Servings.

CHINESE PARTY FRIED RICE

6 oz. (1 c.) Brown Rice
16 oz. Bean Sprouts
2 Eggs
4 oz. (1 c.) peeled Prawns (shrimps)
2 ½ tbsp. Peanut Oil
1 ¼ tbsp. Soy Sauce
4 oz. (1 c.) cooked Chicken
2 c. Water or chicken stock

Cook the rice as per instructions at beginning of this chapter. Cool, cover and place in the refrigerator or a cool place overnight. Wash bean sprouts well under cold water and drain. Cut prawns in half and cut the chicken into strips. Beat the eggs with salt. Heat the oil in a large frying pan. Add the eggs and fry until half set. Add the rice and fry constantly stirring until the rice grains are coated in egg. Keep stirring and turning the rice over and over. Add the prawns (shrimps), chicken, bean sprouts, water or chicken stock and soy sauce. Fry, stirring constantly, for 3-4 minutes. Yield: 4-6 Servings.

30 Days To No More PMS
The Cook Book

VARIATIONS FOR PARTY FRIED RICE:

Omit the bean sprouts, prawns and chicken. Use 1 ½ c. of flaked crab, lobster or tuna meat, 3 chopped shallots and 2 tomatoes (skinned, deseeded and chopped).

VEGETABLE MAIN AND SIDE DISHES

BANANA DELIGHT
2 c. Banana, mashed, cooked
½ c. Orange juice
2 tbsp. Margarine
½ tsp. Salt
Pepper to taste
½ c. Pecans

Heat mashed banana and beat in enough orange juice to the consistency of whipped potatoes. Beat margarine, salt and pepper to taste. Whip until fluffy. Mound in bowl and sprinkle with pecans.

This recipe can be varied by using cashews, peanuts or squash instead of banana. Yield: 6 servings.

BAKED EGGPLANT
1 medium-large Eggplant (1 ½ lb.)
1 lg. Tomato
½ c. Onion, chopped finely
1 clove Garlic
2 tsp. Olive or Safflower Oil
2 tsp. Lemon juice
Salt (preferably Kosher)
Pepper, freshly ground

Preheat oven to 375 degrees. Place whole unpeeled eggplant, pierced with a fork in several places, into a shallow greased baking pan and bake for 30 minutes or until soft. Let cool, peel and finely dice pulp. Drop tomato into pan of boiling water for a few seconds, run under cold water, peel and chop finely. Mince garlic and then with

30 Days To No More PMS
The Cook Book

the side of a large knife, mash it with 1 tsp. salt, preferably coarse kosher salt. Mix all the ingredients; chill well. Serve with whole wheat bread. Yield: 8 servings.

LENTIL NUT LOAF
1 Onion, small chopped fine
3 tbsp. Safflower Oil
½ c. Wheat Germ
2 c. Lentils, cooked drained
½ c. Whole Wheat bread crumbs
½ c. Walnut pieces
½ tsp. Sage or Thyme
2 tbsp. Torula Yeast
2 tbsp. Soy flour
2 Eggs, beaten
½ c. Vegetable stock
1 tbsp. Vinegar

Preheat oven to 350 degrees. Mix ingredients and place in a large, greased loaf pan. Bake for 30 minutes, covered with aluminum foil or a cookie sheet, and then for 10 minutes uncovered. Yield: Serves 6.

WILD RICE DELIGHT

1 c. Wild Rice	1 tsp. Marjoram
21/3 c. Brown Rice	¼ tsp. Rosemary
5 c. Stock or water	¼ tsp. Thyme
1 Carrot	1 tsp. Salt
1 large stalk Celery	a dash Pepper
6 Green Onions	a pinch of Garlic
2 tbsp. Safflower Oil	1/3 c. toasted Almonds

Chop celery and carrots in ¼-inch cubes. Chop green onions and saute' them in margarine. Add stock and bring to a boil. Stir in the remaining ingredients (except almonds). Bring to a boil, cover, reduce heat, and cook gently for an hour or more, until the rice is tender. Chop the almonds and add them about 20 minutes before serving. Yield: 5 cups.

30 Days To No More PMS
The Cook Book

SPANISH RICE

1 c. raw Brown Rice	1 tsp. Salt
1 Onion, minced	½ tsp. Oregano
1 tsp. Safflower Oil	½ tsp. Basil
2 c. Vegetable stock/water	dash of Pepper
4 stalks Celery, diced small	pinch Chili powder
1 large Green Pepper, diced	
3 medium fresh or 1 c. canned Tomatoes, chopped	

Bring the stock, oil, onions, and rice to a boil. Cover and simmer on low heat for 25 minutes Add remaining ingredients. Simmer another 20 minutes or until rice is well cooked. Yield: 4 cups.

RICE LENTIL CASSEROLE

½ Onion, medium	1 tbsp. Tomato paste
3 tbsp. Safflower Oil	1 tsp. Salt
1 c. Brown Rice	½ c. Raisins
¼ c. Lentils	½ c. Cashews, chopped
¼ tsp. Cinnamon	
2 ½ c. Vegetable stock/water	

Chop onion and saute' in 2 tablespoons of the oil until soft. Add rice and cook stirring for several minutes. Combine tomato paste with water and cinnamon. Add this mixture, along with the lentils, to the rice. Bring to a boil, cover tightly, turn heat very low, and simmer for 30 minutes.

Preheat oven to 350 degrees F. Stir in salt, nuts, and raisins. Coat a baking dish with the remaining tablespoon of oil and 1 tablespoon of hot water. Pour in rice mixture. Cover and bake for 20-30 minutes. Yield: 4 to 6 servings.

BULGUR WHEAT PILAF

Pilaf can be made with just about any grain, you can substitute millet, cracked wheat, rice, or triticale or barley in this recipe. You can even make combinations of certain grains such as a 3 grain pilaf, i.e. wheat, millet and barley. Adjust cooking times or cook separately and then combine in step two.

1 3/4 c. Vegetable stock/water   2 Green Onions

30 Days To No More PMS
The Cook Book

1 small Carrot	1 Bay Leaf
1 medium stalk Celery	1 ½ tbsp. Safflower Oil
½ Green Pepper	1 c. Bulgur Wheat
¼ c. chopped Mushroom	1 tsp. Salt

Dice carrot, celery (the leaves can also be used to), green pepper, and onions. Place the oil in a heavy pot with a close-fitting lid. Add all the vegetables and the bay leaf and stir over medium heat for several minutes. Pour in the stock, bring to a boil, and simmer for 5 minutes, covered.

Add wheat and salt and bring to fast boil again. Cook, covered, over very low heat for 15 minutes. If too moist, uncover and simmer another few minutes until liquid diminishes.

This recipe can be varied in many ways to use as a main dish by adding chicken, turkey or beef chunks. For special occasions add 1 cup garden peas towards the very end of the cooking time, and ¼ cup toasted chopped cashews. Yield: 4-6 servings.

TAMALE PIE

2 c. cooked Pinto or Kidney Beans	2 tbsp. Safflower Oil
½ c. chopped Onions	¼ tsp. Garlic powder
1 tsp. Chili powder	1 tsp. Salt
1 tbsp. Tomato paste	3 tbsp Water
¼ c. sliced ripe Olives	½ c. fresh Corn
½ Green Pepper, chopped	½ c chopped Celery

Grind the beans in blender or mash in food mill. Mix tomato paste with water. In a skillet saute' onions in oil and combine all above. Let these cook over medium heat; if the beans were hot to begin with then no more than 5 minutes cooking is usually needed. Keep stirring the mixture since beans tend to stick to the pan. Add seasonings to taste.

Combine the following ingredients, except for cheese, into a heavy pan and cook over

2 ½ c. cold Water	1 ½ c. Cornmeal
1 tsp. Salt	½ tsp. Chili powder
¼ c. grated Cheddar Cheese (if calcium is not your problem)	

medium heat until cornmeal thickens and comes to a boil. You have to stir constantly or the cornmeal will stick.

Grease an 8"x 8" pan and spread two thirds of the cornmeal mixture over the bottom and sides; then pour the bean mixture into the cornmeal crust and spread the remaining one third of the cornmeal on the top. Sprinkle the top crust with grated cheddar cheese and cook in a 350 degree oven for half an hour. Yield: 6-8 servings.

KICHADI

2 c. Brown Rice	2 tsp. ground Fenugreek Seeds
2 Cloves	2 Onions
1 very small Cinnamon stick	1 Green Pepper
Cardamom Seeds from 3 pods	4 tbsp. Safflower Oil
a dash Turmeric powder	6 c. Water
1 c. Yellow Split Peas	2 tsp. Salt

Saute' spices in 2 tablespoons oil, in a large, heavy-bottomed pot. If the spices are not available, use 2 teaspoons of curry powder instead. Add finely chopped onions and green pepper and stir until onions are soft.

Stir in the rice and continue to cook for about 5 minutes, or until rice begins to turn white. Add water and salt and bring to a boil. Cover and cook on low heat for 20 minutes. If dry split peas are used, cook 1 hour.

Saute' yellow split peas in remaining 2 tablespoons oil. Add split peas to the cooking rice and continue cooking for 30 minutes more. Yield: 6 cups.

HERBS AND SPICES

For the PMS woman there is a definite reduction of the varieties of foods which she can eat. This demands a certain amount of creativity. Since creativity is often limited in respect to the varieties of foods she can eat, creativity must come through changing the tastes of foods. This can best be done by using herbs and spices. The challenge for the PMS woman is to learn to vary her menu without having to use foods high in calcium, sugar, processed foods, preservatives or additives. The foods chosen should, as best as possible, have a magnesium/calcium ratio of 2/1 or greater.

30 Days To No More PMS
The Cook Book

We will now give some basic information about herbs and spices. What you will need to do is to expand on this information by experimenting with the herbs and spices. In the recipes given in this book we have liberally used herbs and spices, you may vary them as you see fit. You may desire to create your own recipes. Please do this and enjoy!

We have little information regarding the amounts of magnesium and calcium that are to be found in herbs and spices. We do know that some are particularly high in calcium. For example, parsley and sesame seeds should be avoided, as much as is possible. Another suggestion would be to use all herbs and spices in moderation.

HERBS

The flavor of fresh herbs is often much superior to dried herbs. Many supermarkets have fresh herbs in their produce sections.

ANISE: Seeds can be used in teas. Gives a licorice flavor. Chinese star anise has an even more pronounced flavor. To release flavor crush seeds between towels with rolling pin.

BASIL: A royal herb, marvelous in tomato and fish dishes. Should be used as fresh as is possible. Add in all savory dishes.

BAY LEAF: A small piece is usually enough in a soup, stew or fish dish. Use fresh or dry, but with discretion-- only 1/3 of a fresh leaf or 1/6 of a dry leaf in a quart of stew and only a pinch in the powdered form. Use in stocks, sauces, marinades and in the cooking of vegetables and meats.

CARAWAY: Use leaves of this herb sparingly in soups, and stews. The seeds, have a flavor similar to cumin. Crush the seeds before adding them to vegetables or salads.

CAYENNE: Cayenne is a pepper and it is very hot, so use only a pinch.

30 Days To No More PMS
The Cook Book

CELERIES: The tender leaves of this herb can be used fresh or dried in almost all foods. Celery salt is a powdered form combined with salt. The seeds either whole or ground, have a powerful flavor and must be used sparingly: whole in stocks, court bouillon, and salads; the ground form in salad dressings, sea foods or vegetables.

CHILIES: Chilies are used fresh or ground. Mix with cumin, garlic, oregano and coriander for chili powder.

COMFREY: A healing herb-- its very name implies a knitting together. Use its young leaves sparingly, raw in salads or cook them with vegetables.

CORIANDER: Fresh leaves may be called Chinese or Mexican parsley or cilantro. Use the whole leaves, no stems, in pea soup, stews and poaching liquids. Coriander seeds freshly ground are pungent in stews, curries and rice dishes. Place on top of roasts.

CUMIN: The seeds can be used whole in marinades, chilies and tomato sauces. Used in curries, bean or rice dishes.

DILL: Both seeds and leaf can be used in fish, beans, cucumber, potato dishes. Try a few seeds in salad vinegar.

FENNEL: The leaves and seeds are used in fish, lentils, grain, rice and potato dishes. Use fresh as when dried its flavor is lost.

FENUGREEK: This has the same odor as celery. The flavor is bitter. It's a main ingredient in curries.

HORSERADISH: Grate fresh root into lemon juice or vinegar and use with fish, potatoes, shellfish and cold meats. It is bitter in taste.

MARJORAM: Very pungent. Great with tomatoes, stews, soup and salads. Use with lamb, pork, chicken and goose. When used in salads use fresh and chop them.

30 Days To No More PMS
The Cook Book

OREGANO: Very pungent. Great with tomatoes, stews, soup and salads. Use with lamb, pork, chicken and goose. When used in salads use fresh and chop them.

MINT: All the mints can be used for teas. Good with peas, salads, cucumbers and rice dishes. They can be used with zucchini, lamb, veal, or as a garnish. Use fresh crushed leaves, ¼ to ½ tsp. In the oil form 1 drop will do.

MUSTARD: Freshly ground seeds taste best, a dash is good in salad dressings. Commercial mustards may use sugar, wine or flour in blending. They should be avoided in sensitive PMS women. Mix your own use 2 to 3 tbsp. liquid to ¼ cup dry mustard, vinegar, rice vinegar or lemon or other spices can be added. Dry mustard is strong so use carefully!

ONION FAMILY: Chives, garlic, shallots, leeks, scallions, onions-red, white or Bermuda. Use them fresh or dried, good in soups, salads, cooked in meats vegetables or on their own.

PARSLEY: This herb is high in calcium and should be avoided by PMS women. Watch for it in recipes!

PEPPERS, RED and GREEN: Rich in magnesium especially the green. Also an excellent source of A and C. Use as a vegetable or as a seasoning. They have bacteria deterrent and anti-oxidant qualities that extend the keeping period of fats, meats and casseroles which include peppers. Seeds and membranes are irritating and should be removed.

PAPRIKA: Paprika is ground from certain dry red peppers. If you use it in cooking add it near the end as it loses flavor when heated. Good for adding color on fish, fowl or meats.

ROSEMARY: Pungent and must be used cautiously. In marinades use ⅛ to ¼ tsp. for every 4 servings. Use crushed leaves sparsely with lamb, duck, capon and veal. It can be used with peas.

30 Days To No More PMS
The Cook Book

SAFFRON:	Use tiny amounts to flavor rice dishes.
SAGE:	Used with fatty meats like pork, duck, and goose. Use fresh as dried loses flavor.
SAVORY:	Summer savory is delicious with lentil soup, potatoes, fish, tomatoes and salad dressing.
SESAME SEEDS:	Do not use as it is extremely high in calcium.
TARRAGON:	Store fresh tarragon in vinegar, flavors the vinegar for salads. You can use the leaves with mushrooms, tomatoes, and fish. When using dry leaves they do not soften with cooking and must be strained out before food is served. Do not crowd leaves in vinegar use 3 tbsp. of dry leaves to 1 quart mild vinegar, this keeps leaves from spoiling.
THYMES:	Use sparingly with poultry, mutton, veal, and in creole and gumbo dishes. Use with fat fish, stews and most vegetables. Can be used in soups and as a garnish.
FINE HERBS:	A good combination of herbs-- usually thyme, basil, tarragon and savory. A cut garlic clove with this makes a good salad dressing seasoning. Oil and vinegar blend is excellent.

SPICES

Whenever possible you should use freshly ground whole spices for best flavor. A small Moulinex type (coffee) grinder works well. Most spices are high in calcium and should be used only in small amounts.

ALLSPICE:	Combines flavors of cinnamon, clove, nutmeg, and allspice. Try in soups and with cooked grains.
ALMOND EXTRACT:	Gives an almond flavor to fruits, can be used with rice and grains for nutty flavor.

30 Days To No More PMS
The Cook Book

CARDAMON: Grind fresh to retain full flavor. Use whole for poaching liquids. Use as for cinnamon and cloves. Delicious in coffee and can be used with decaffeinated coffee.

CINNAMON: Most cinnamon is really cassia, slightly more bitter than true cinnamon. Use in stick form in teas, try small amounts ground in stews and bean dishes, use a dash with squash, carrots, and sweet potatoes. Use on whole wheat toast sprinkled for a new taste. Add to deserts. Use in protein malts.

CLOVES: Use in teas, curries and stews. Cloves are high in magnesium. Always remove whole cloves cooked within foods before serving.

CURRY: Freshly ground curry powders are superior in flavor. Try in vegetables, bean and fish dishes with fresh onions and garlic. Can be used to curry fruits such as apples or carrots. Curry either in powder or paste form, has its flavor developed in olive oil. Curries should be especially blended for each kind of dish: a dry one for coating meat; a sour one for marinated meats. It can be used with chicken, mutton, rice, beans, vegetables and fish. When making up the dish, use plenty of fresh garlic and onion and, if possible, fresh coconut milk.

GINGER: Grate fresh ginger, add to stews or fish as you would garlic. Try ginger on grain and bean dishes. Ginger is low in calcium.

NUTMEG & MACE: From the same fruit. Freshly ground nutmeg from a grinder like a pepper mill is wonderful on grains, carrots, yellow squash and sweet potatoes. Use sparingly but often.

30 Days To No More PMS
The Cook Book

WHITE or BLACK PEPPER: Best freshly ground. Use sparingly.

POPPY SEEDS: Can be ground to release full flavor. Sprinkle on fruit salad.

TURMERIC: Strong use in small amounts. Gives yellow color to curry powder.

VANILLA BEAN and EXTRACT: Do not use synthetic vanilla. A few drops are great in drinks such as protein malts. Generally contains alcohol so use carefully.

SPICE MIX
1 tbsp. Cardamon Seeds
1 tsp. Cloves
1 tsp. Black Peppercorn
1 tsp. Cumin Seeds
1/3 of a Nutmeg
1 ½ in. stick Cinnamon

Grind in a coffee grinder.

FRESH CURRY POWDER
Seeds, 2 oz. each:
  Black Pepper
  Coriander
  Fenugreek
  Turmeric
2 ½ oz. Cumin Seeds
1 ½ oz. each Cardamon, Poppy Seeds
½ oz. Mustard Seeds
½ oz. dry Ginger
2 oz. dry Chili
1 oz. Cinnamon

Grind in small grinder. Store in tightly closed jar.

30 Days To No More PMS
The Cook Book

SALSA # 1
2 c. lime or lemon juice
1 c. jicama, grated coarsely
½ onion, finely chopped
½ c. cilantro leaves, finely chopped
1 green chili, seeded, finely chopped

SALSA #2:
5 c. tomatoes, chopped
1 c. cilantro leaves, finely chopped
¼ c. red onion, finely chopped
¼ tsp. hot pepper, finely chopped

Serve either salsa on fish, chicken or turkey. Salsa can also be served on whole grains such as brown rice, millet or buckwheat.

BREADS, ROLLS AND CAKES

Few meals are complete without bread, rolls or some baked goods. Every woman must yield to the temptation of some breads in her diet. No one could have a sandwich, toast or even croutons in a salad without bread. However, there are some breads which are *bad for you* and there are breads which are *Good for you*. We discussed the parameters earlier but we will review them for you once again. Avoid refined products and avoid sugar. Maximize the whole grains which are high in magnesium and if you need sweetness, sweeten with fruit or fruit juices. Another suggestion is to avoid butter and fats either in or on the baked goods. Watch dairy and calcium levels (cream, milk, buttermilk, cheese, butter, preservatives with calcium, see Appendix 3, Foods To Avoid - Foods High In Calcium).

CARROT LOAF
1 ½ c. Safflower oil
1 c. Rice Syrup
1 c. Apple juice
4 Eggs
1 c. Unbleached all-purpose Flour
1 c. less 2 tablespoons Whole-wheat flour
1 tsp. Salt

30 Days To No More PMS
The Cook Book

2 tsp. Baking soda
2 tsp. Baking powder
2 tsp. Cinnamon, ground
1 ½ c. Carrots, finely shredded raw
4 ½ ounces Pineapple, crushed and drained
2 ½ c. Banana, mashed
½ c. Cashews, finely chopped (optional)

In a large bowl blend together the safflower oil, rice syrup and apple juice. Add eggs one at a time, beating until blended. In another bowl sift together both flours, salt, soda, baking powder and cinnamon. Add the flour mixture, about 1/3 at a time, to the oil mixture, beating just enough to blend. Next add the carrots, banana and then the pineapple to the batter. Add the cashews if desired. Pour the batter into 2 greased and lightly floured loaf pans. Bake in a preheated 350 degree oven for 35-40 minutes or until a toothpick inserted into the center comes out clean. Cool the loaves in the pans on a rack for 10 minutes. Turn loaves out on the rack and cool completely. For storage loaves may be wrapped in airtight plastic wrap and refrigerated for 5-6 days or frozen for 2-3 months.

NATURAL BRAN MUFFINS
1 c. Whole bran cereal (health food store type) without sugar
1 c. boiling Water
1 ½ c. Vegetable Oil (Corn oil, Safflower oil, etc.)
1 c. Apple juice, frozen concentrate unsweetened
½ c. Orange juice
2 Eggs
2 ½ c. Whole-Wheat Flour
2 ½ tsp. Baking soda
1 tsp. Salt
2 c. Granola (see recipe in Snack section)

In a 2-3 quart container or bowl with a cover stir together the bran and water. Let stand for 10 minutes or until the water is absorbed. In another bowl combine the oil, apple juice and orange juice. Mix well. Beat the eggs into the oil mixture. In another bowl combine and mix flour, soda, salt and granola. Slowly blend these ingredients into the bran mixture. Cover and refrigerate the batter for several hours or overnight. Remove enough batter to make desired amount of muffins. Spoon the

30 Days To No More PMS
The Cook Book

batter into greased muffin tins, ½-2/3 full. Bake in a preheated 400 degree oven for 20-25 minutes or until well browned and a toothpick inserted in the center of a muffin comes out clean. Serve warm. NOTE: The remaining batter may be used as needed and will keep refrigerated, tightly sealed, for 4 weeks.

Variations: Before baking, add chopped, unpeeled pippin apples, chopped cashews and/or mashed banana to the batter in whatever amounts desired. For the 2 cups granola, a combination of bran, oatmeal and a small amount of wheat germ or just adding more bran-all totaling 2 cups.

WHOLE WHEAT BREAD
3 c. lukewarm Water (110 degrees)
¼ c. Apple juice, unsweetened concentrate at room temperature
2 pkg. Active dry yeast
¼ c. Safflower Oil
7-10 c. Stone Ground Whole-Wheat Flour
2 tsp. Salt

In a very large mixing bowl combine and mix the lukewarm water, apple juice and yeast until the yeast is softened, about 5 minutes. Blend the safflower oil, whole-wheat flour and salt into the yeast mixture. Beat the mixture by hand (at least 100 strokes) or with an electric mixer on low speed for 7 minutes. Slowly add 2 or 3 cups whole-wheat flour, beating with a wooden spoon, until a stiff dough is formed.

Sprinkle 1 cup of the remaining flour on a breadboard, turn the dough out on the board, and knead, continuing to add flour if the dough is sticky. Knead 8-10 minutes or until the dough is smooth and elastic. Place it, smooth side down, in a greased bowl and turn the dough to grease its top. Cover the bowl with a damp towel and place it in a warm (80-85 degree) draft-free place until the dough has doubled in bulk, about 1 hour.

Knead the dough down for 1 minute, cover, and let rise in a warm place again, until doubled (probably less than the amount of time required for the first rising; it will vary with the temperature and brand of flour used).

Punch down a second time, divide the dough in half, shape in 2 loaves, and place in greased 9 X 5 inch loaf pans. Put in a warm place and allow to rise to the top of the

30 Days To No More PMS
The Cook Book

pans (possibly 45 minutes). Bake the loaves in a preheated 350 degree oven for about 1 hour or until they are well browned and hollow-sounding when the tops are tapped. Turn loaves out on a rack to cool.

QUICK CORN MUFFINS
1 c. Yellow Cornmeal (ungerminated)
1 c. Whole Wheat Flour
1 tbsp. Baking powder
½ tsp. Baking Soda
½ tsp. Salt
¼ c. Safflower Oil
4 tbsp. Apple juice, unsweetened concentrate
3 Eggs
1 c. Banana, mashed

Stir together dry ingredients and set aside. Blend oil, apple juice, eggs, and banana with a fork. Stir into dry ingredients. Spoon into paper-lined muffin cups. Bake 20-25 minutes in preheated 375 degree oven. Yield: 12 Muffins.

DESSERTS

To many of us dessert is the most important part of the meal. For the PMS woman it can be the most dangerous part of the meal. Here again we must remind you of the major problems of PMS-- sugar, calcium and caffeine. Most desserts have some combinations of these.

You must recognize that ice cream, sherbet, cookies, cakes, candies, coffee, espresso, alcoholic beverages are made up of various combinations of sugar, calcium and caffeine. How does one get around this major disaster? There is, of course no easy answer. There is instead a desire to be symptom free, a sense of will-power and discipline. You will again have to become creative!

DATE-NUT BARS
3 Eggs, slightly beaten, you can also use egg substitute
2 c. Dates, pitted
1 c. Pecans or Cashews
1 tsp. Baking powder

30 Days To No More PMS
The Cook Book

¼ c. Banana, mashed
1 c. Whole Wheat Flour
¼ c. Apple juice, frozen concentrate
½ c. Bran (or ¼ c. bran and ¼ c. wheat germ)

Combine eggs with all other ingredients. Line a 9 x 13 inch pan with waxed paper. Spread batter in pan. (It may look like not enough to cover the nuts and dates, but it will spread and rise as it bakes.) Preheat oven to 250 degrees. Bake for approximately 35 minutes. Remove from oven and allow to cool (10 minutes.) Turn pan over, face down and peel off waxed paper. Cool for an additional 20 minutes, then cut into rectangular bars. To store, wrap tightly in plastic wrap or in an airtight container. Yield: 2 dozen

BANANA RAISIN COOKIES
3 Bananas
½ c. chopped Nuts (pecans, cashews, almonds)
1/3 c. Vegetable oil
½ c. Raisins, chopped
½ tsp. Salt
1 tsp. Vanilla
2 c. Oatmeal

Mix all ingredients and let stand until moisture is absorbed. Drop by small spoonfuls on ungreased cookie sheet. Bake in preheated 350 degree oven for 20 to 25 minutes. Yield: 3 dozen

BANANA CRUNCHIES
3/4 c. Orange juice or Apple juice
3 Bananas
½ c. chopped salt free Nuts, wheat germ or bran

Peel and cut bananas into 1 inch slices. Using a fork, dip in juice, then roll in nuts or wheat germ. May be frozen. Yield: 20 pieces

CARROT PUDDING
1 c. Whole Wheat Flour
¼ tsp. Salt

30 Days To No More PMS
The Cook Book

1 tsp. Baking soda
½ tsp. Allspice
½ tsp. Cloves, ground
1 c. grated raw Potato
3/4 c. grated raw Carrots
½ c. Safflower Oil
3/4 c. frozen Apple juice concentrate
½ c. chopped Pecans, Cashews or Peanuts

Sift dry ingredients together. Combine with carrots and potatoes. Add safflower oil, apple juice and nuts. Mix well and put on a greased pan. Steam 3 ½ hours. Serve with lemon juice. Yield: 6 servings

SAMPAN PUDDING
1 ½ c. Tofu, drained and crumbled
½ c. crunchy natural Peanut Butter
1 ½ Bananas
Juice of ½ Lemon or tbsp.
3-4 Ice cubes
1 ½ tbsp. frozen concentrate Apple juice
1 tbsp. Carob powder, unsweetened (optional)
1 tbsp. unsweetened shredded Coconut as garnish (optional)

Combine all ingredients except optional coconut in a blender and puree until smooth or until ice disappears. Pour into sherbet glasses or dessert dishes and chill. Add coconut before serving. VARIATION: Freeze until mixture begins to crystallize. Stir and serve. Yield: 2 to 4 servings.

FROZEN BANANA OR PERSIMMONS
Peel a ripe banana. Cut in halves, thirds or chunks. Put the pieces on a stick if you wish. Drop in a baggy, seal and freeze. In a couple hours, a delicious treat will be waiting for you.

PINEAPPLE FREEZE
Freeze one 8 oz. can of pineapple in its own juice (no sugar). Pour into an ice cube tray so that the pieces are evenly distributed.

30 Days To No More PMS
The Cook Book

FRUIT SALAD

A liberal assortment of fresh fruits peaches, oranges, apples, nectarines, berries: strawberries, black berries, raspberries, blue berries, etc. In fact, you can use any fruit in season. Cut fruit into pieces in large bowel. A can of chunk pineapple in its own juice will blend all of the ingredients together.

FRESH FRUITS AND NUTS

We will list fresh fruits and nuts in order of from most valuable to least valuable.

BEST - MOST VALUABLE - High In Magnesium:
Black walnuts
Cashews
Bananas, dried
Coconut meats, dried or fresh
Peanuts
Bananas, fresh
Nectarines

FAIR:
Pecans
Mangoes

ONLY AFTER HIGH MAGNESIUM MEAL:
Grapefruits
Persimmon, Japanese
Walnuts, English
Pistachio nuts
Brazil nuts
Almonds
Peaches, fresh
Watermelon
Apples
Cantaloupe

30 Days To No More PMS
The Cook Book

Black Raspberry
Dates

BEVERAGES

Beverages are another problem, as with desserts they so often contain sugar or dairy products. Drinks can come in two types: light, such as water, mineral water, diet sodas, and fruit juice; or heavy, such as blended juices or protein drinks. In general there are few choices of drinks that are low in sugar, low in calcium and high in magnesium and without caffeine.

Here are a few suggestions:

Water:
One should not forget the best of all drinks. Water, yes, just plain water directly out of the tap, bottled, filtered, hot or cold. It has no calories, no ingredients that would worse PMS and can be taken with or without meals. It can be used alone or with a twist of lemon or lime.

Fruit Juices:
Any fruit juice can be used as a beverage. The can be prepared alone or in combinations. For example: Apple juice, grape juice, grapefruit juice, orange juice, lemon juice, lime juice, etc.

Combinations such as: grape and apple juice, orange and banana blended together, lemon and lime juices, Coconut juice and apple juice and banana, etc.

Be creative, consider diluting enough so that it tastes good but has the least amount of calories.

Soda water:
This can be obtained from bottled carbonated water and or mineral water. You can make soda water yourself with a soda syphon and CO_2 cartridges.

Soda water and fruit juice mixture:
Using soda water, mix small amounts of juices: grapefruit, coconut milk, lemon juice, lime juice, or a favorite of ours, unsweetened cranberry juice. Only small amounts of these juices are needed, a teaspoon or a few drops, just enough to flavor. The amount used should not be enough to be the main element of these drinks.

30 Days To No More PMS
The Cook Book

Diet Drinks:

Although these are easy and appear to be a good choice, we generally recommend against them because of the number of artificial ingredients. When symptoms are in good control they can be used more liberally.

Herb Teas:

Herb teas are excellent drinks for the PMS woman. They should be taken without sugar, and they can be used either hot or cold. Stay away from non-herbal commercial teas (see Appendix 4) because of caffeine.

Decaffeinated Coffee:

Choose your decaffeinated coffee carefully. Swiss water dissolved decaffeinated is best *(Read the label of the coffee can*, if it does not say *Swiss* or *water* decaffeinated, *it is not*. Generally watch carefully to see if it causes or worsens PMS symptoms. Can be used hot or cold.

Blended Drinks:

Fresh fruits (see list above) in various combinations can be blended with protein powder. The protein powder should be scrutinized for its calcium content, those high in calcium should be avoided.

Here are some recipes for your use:

SPECIAL EYE OPENER (SMOOTHIE)
½ c. Tofu, well drained and crumbled
½ c. unsweetened concentrated Apple juice or Grapefruit juice
1 tbsp. Lemon juice (or to taste)
½ Banana, sliced
3-4 Ice cubes

Combine all ingredients in blender and blend until smooth, or until ice has dissolved. Serve immediately. Preparation time: 10 minutes. Yield: One regular or two small servings.

ICED HERBAL TEA
This is a great summer drink.
1 tsp. Decaffeinated tea or one Herb tea bag for each cup water

30 Days To No More PMS
The Cook Book

1 tsp. Apple juice or Rice syrup for each cup water (optional)

Decide how many cups of iced tea you want to make. Extra tea will stay fresh for a few days if you keep it in the refrigerator. When you have decided how many cups you wish to make, boil the water. After the water boils, either steep or boil the tea, depending on the kind of tea you are using. Raspberry leaf, camomile, mint and strawberry leaf teas don't require boiling. Just place in a strainer and soak it in freshly boiled water for about 3 minutes. When you use teas made out of tree bark or twigs such as sassafras or bancha, place in teaball and let it cook in gently boiling water for about 10 minutes. Use ½ tsp. tea for each cup of water.) Use herb tea bag the same as a regular tea bag. Add the apple juice, rice syrup or artificial sweetener if you feel you need sweet tea. (Try to get used to drinking beverages with as little sweetening as possible.) Mix tea well. Pour it into a pitcher. Place in refrigerator for about an hour to chill. Add 2 or 3 ice cubes to each glass or put the ice cubes in a pitcher. Pour in the tea. Serve.

MU TEA WINTER WARMUP
Mu tea is a tea that is made up from sixteen different herbs and is very full bodied. Use sparingly as a little goes a long way. This tea is available in health food stores. Mu tea tastes best served hot and on cold winter mornings it is a welcome warmup.

1 Mu tea bag
4 cups Water
¼ - ½ c. Apple juice
Pinch of Cinnamon or 1 Cinnamon stick

Boil water. Drop the tea bag in the water. Let it simmer for 5 minutes. Remove tea bag carefully with a spoon. Add apple juice to sweeten. Continue heating for about 3 minutes on a medium flame. Mix in the cinnamon (a pinch for one serving or float a cinnamon stick in a pitcher of Mu tea.) Yield: About 4-5 cups.

BREAKFAST DISHES

You can take from any of the prior recipes for your breakfast. You can have a steak, chicken or left over Turkey Roll. If you would rather have a more traditional breakfast check out the following recipes.

30 Days To No More PMS
The Cook Book

EGG WHITE OMELET CALIFORNIA
4 Egg whites (Egg Beater or equivalent is also okay)
¼ c. Onions, chopped
¼ c. Yellow corn, kernels only
¼ c. Avocado, cut into pieces
2 tbsp. Garlic, crushed
1 tsp. Italian herbs
Salt and pepper to taste
Worcestershire Sauce

Heat frying pan can either be Teflon, or use a small amount of canola or other vegetable oil, add egg white, salt and pepper, Worcestershire sauce, mix and then and let it form into an omelet. Once omelet is formed add additional vegetables, tomato or any other vegetables you like such as spinach, tomatoes, cauliflower, celery, etc. Flip omelet and let second side cook until browned.

Add seasoning to eggs or to vegetables as you cook. For a treat serve this dish with Cottage Fried Potatoes below.

COTTAGE FRIED POTATOES
1 large potato, with skin
Teflon Pan or canola or other vegetable oil
Salt and pepper

Wash and then cut potatoes into thin slices.
Warm frying pan, heat oil
Add salt and pepper
Add potatoes and fry to golden brown.
Drain potatoes of excess oil either on rack or paper towel on the dish they will be served on.

BREAKFAST CEREAL DELIGHT
½ cup of any of the following cereals: Kellogg's All-Bran, Post bran Flakes, Kellogg's Mini-Wheats, with Raisins, Kellogg Complete, (wheat or Oats) Kellogg's raisin Bran, Quaker Harvest Crunch
1 tbsp. Corn Germ, toasted
1 tbsp. Kretschmer's Wheat Bran, toasted

30 Days To No More PMS
The Cook Book

Mix together and serve with skim milk.

For a variation mix all or some of the above listed cereals (see information about Grain in Appendices 1, 2, 6, 8, 9 and 11) of the above together and use ½ cup, Corn germ and Wheat Bran along with skim Milk. Add any fruit, especially banana, dehydrated pineapple in chunks or slices to taste. Plums, peaches, whole pineapple, and berries are also okay in smaller amounts. For additional treat add cashew nuts or pumpkin seeds, This can be eaten cold or hot.

Chose from any of the higher magnesium cereals found in the Appendix 11 Fiber section, use non-fat or low fat milk. Serve hot or cold.

CHAPTER 2

SAMPLE MENUS

In order to fully utilize the recipes we have given to you, we suggest that you create a two week menu for yourself. The following is a sample of what it could look like. Vary the foods according to your personal likes and dislikes. Give yourself enough variety to enjoy what you eat. Finally, vary the foods according to your needs to relieve your symptoms.[*]

/ SUNDAY /

Breakfast: Special Eye Opener Drink
Natural Bran Muffin

Mid-morning: 3/4 c. Fruit and Nut Snack Mix
1 or more glasses of Water

Lunch: Jicama Sandwich
¼ c. Guacamole
½ c. Vegetable Gumbo Soup

Mid-afternoon: 1 Orange
1 Quick Corn Muffin
Water or selection from the beverage section.

Dinner: Roast Duck
Wild Rice Stuffing
Carrot sticks
Sliced nectarine on a bed of lettuce with 6 raw cashews
Water or selection from the beverage section.

/ MONDAY /

Breakfast: 1 Orange or Nectarine
3/4 cup cooked Whole Grain Cereal (buckwheat, millet, oats, 7-Grain cereals)
1 tsp. Raisin
Herb tea

30 Days To No More PMS
The Cook Book

Mid-morning: 1 Apple
6-8 raw Cashews
1 or more glasses of Water

Lunch: Salad: shredded Cabbage, Lettuce, Alfalfa Sprouts, Mushrooms, ¼ Avocado
1 tbsp. oil, add vinegar and herbs to taste
1 slice Whole Grain Bread
Water or selection from the beverage section.

Mid-afternoon: ½ cup Puffed Cereal
½ to 1 Banana
1 or more glasses of Water

Dinner: Easy Fish (4-6 oz.)
Onions and Mushrooms, stir-fry in soy sauce
Baked Potato with 1 tsp. margarine
Pepper Slaw
Water or selection from the beverage section.

/ TUESDAY /

Breakfast: 1 Apple
1 Egg scrambled in ½ tsp. margarine
1 slice Whole Wheat Bread
Herb tea

Mid-morning: 1 Banana
1 Rice cake
1 or more glasses of Water

Lunch: 3 oz. can water packed Tuna
1-2 Tomatoes, Celery, Water Chestnuts
3-4 Finn Crisp crackers
dressing for tuna: 1-2 tbsp. Homemade Mayonnaise
Water or selection from the beverage section.

30 Days To No More PMS
The Cook Book

Mid-afternoon: ½ - 3/4 c. Easy No Sugar Granola
1 or more glasses of Water

Dinner: Cuban Black Beans and rice
Cucumber Salad with Green Pepper in
1 tbsp. Safflower oil
Unlimited vinegar and herbs
¼ c. lightly cooked Carrots
Water or selection from the beverage section.

/ WEDNESDAY /

Breakfast: 3/4 c. cooked Cereal (oats, wheat or millet)
1 banana
Decaffeinated coffee (water process when possible)

Mid-morning: 1 slice Whole Grain Bread
1 tsp. raw Almond Butter
1 or more glasses of Water

Lunch: 1 c. Vegetable Barley Mushroom Delight Soup
2-3 whole grain crackers
1 medium Tomato sliced with Mushrooms in vinaigrette
Water or selection from the beverage section.

Mid-afternoon: 2-4 Crab Stuffed Mushroom Caps
1 Rice cake
1 or more glasses of Water

Dinner: 2 Stuffed Chicken Legs
Mushroom-Sprout Delight
1 Quick Corn Muffin
Water or selection from the beverage section.

/ THURSDAY /

Breakfast: Snow Capped Quarters
½ Grapefruit

30 Days To No More PMS
The Cook Book

                  Mu Tea Winter Warmup

Mid-morning: 1 Nectarine
½ c. High Energy Snack Mix
1 or more glasses of Water

Lunch: Salad in a Sandwich
Water or selection from the beverage section.

Mid-afternoon: 2-3 Banana Raisin Cookies
Decaffeinated coffee

Dinner: 3/4 -1 c. Vegetable Barley Mushroom Delight Soup
3-4 oz. Baked Red Snapper
Steamed Corn on the cob
Water or selection from the beverage section.

/ FRIDAY /

Breakfast: 3/4 - 1 cup cooked Whole Grain Cereal (millet, buckwheat, oats)
1 tsp. Margarine
1 grated Apple
Herb tea

Mid-morning: ½ Grapefruit
1 or more glasses of Water

Lunch: Avocado Delight
2 slices Tomato
4 slices Cucumber
Water or selection from the beverage section.

Mid-afternoon: 1 Natural Bran Muffin
1 or more glasses of Water

Dinner: Fish with Zucchini
baked Yellow Squash

30 Days To No More PMS
The Cook Book

                 medium baked Potato
                 Water or selection from the beverage section.

/ SATURDAY /

Breakfast: 1 c. Black Raspberries
                 Whole Grain Crackers with 1-2 tbsp. peanut butter
                 Decaffeinated coffee

Mid-morning: 1 Nectarine
                 6-8 raw Cashews
                 1 or more glasses of Water

Lunch: Tuna Delight on Whole wheat bread
                 1 Apple
                 Herb tea

Mid-afternoon: Banana smoothie = $\frac{1}{8}$ c. orange juice, 1 banana
                 Water and ice cubes, blended
                 1 Rice cake

Dinner: Chicken Nani
                 Steamed Brown Rice
                 ½ c. Lima Beans
                 Tomato slices with Mushroom slices and
                 Vinaigrette dressing
                 Water or selection from the beverage section.

* The sample menu above is just that a SAMPLE menu it is included to stimulate you to create a one to two week menu which will please your tastes. We encourage you strongly to use the recipes from this book. You, of course are also encouraged to be creative and make up your own recipes. Remember the principles 1) high magnesium 2) low calcium 3) eliminate sugars, processed foods, additives, preservatives and fats, 4) Fresh foods whenever possible.

30 Days To No More PMS
The Cook Book

ONE WEEK SAMPLE MENU

	Sunday	Monday	Tuesday	Wednesday	Thursday	Friday	Saturday
Breakfast	Special Eye Opener Drink Natural Bran Muffin	1 Orange or Nectarine 3/4 cup cooked Whole Grain Cereal (buckwheat, millet, oats, 7-Grain cereals) 1 tsp. Raisin Herb tea	1 Apple 1 Egg scrambled in ½ tsp. margarine 1 slice Whole Wheat Bread Herb tea	3/4 c. cooked Cereal (oats, wheat or millet) 1 banana decaffeinated coffee (water process when possible)	Snow Capped Quarters ½ Grapefruit Mu Tea Winter Warmup	3/4 - 1 cup cooked Whole Grain Cereal (millet, buckwheat, oats) 1 tsp. Margarine 1 grated Apple Herb tea	1 c. Black Raspberries Whole Grain Crackers with 1-2 tbsp. peanut butter Decaffeinated coffee
Snack	3/4 c. Fruit and Nut SnackMix 1 or more glasses of Water	1 Apple 6-8 raw Cashews 1 or more glasses of Water	1 Banana 1 Rice cake 1 or more glasses of Water	1 slice Whole Grain Bread 1 tsp. raw Almond Butter 1 or more glasses of Water	1 Nectarine ½ c. High Energy Snack Mix 1 or more glasses of Water	½ Grapefruit 1 or more glasses of Water	1 Nectarine 6-8 raw Cashews 1 or more glasses of Water
Lunch	Jicama Sandwich 1/4 c. Guacamole ½ c. Vegetable Gumbo Soup	Salad: shredded Cabbage, Lettuce, Alfalfa Sprouts, Mushrooms, 1/4 Avocado 1 tbsp. oil, add vinegar and herbs to taste 1 slice Whole Grain Bread Water or selection from the beverage section	3 oz. can water packed Tuna 1-2 Tomatoes, Celery, Water Chestnuts 3-4 Crisp crackers Dressing for tuna: 1-2 tbsp. Homemade Mayonnaise Water or selection from the beverage section.	1 c. Vegetable Barley Mushroom Delight Soup 2-3 whole grain crackers 1 medium Tomato sliced with Mushrooms in vinaigrette Water or selection from the beverage section	Salad in a Sandwich Water or selection from the beverage section	Avocado Delight 2 slices Tomato 4 slices Cucumber Water or selection from the beverage section.	Tuna Delight on Whole wheat bread 1 Apple Herb tea

30 Days To No More PMS
The Cook Book

Snack	1 Orange 1 Quick Corn Muffin Water or selection from the beverage section.	½ cup Puffed Cereal ½ to 1 Banana 1 or more glasses of Water	½ - 3/4 c. Easy No Sugar Granola 1 or more glasses of Water	2-4 Crab Stuffed Mushroom Caps 1 Rice cake 1 or more glasses of Water	2-3 Banana Raisin Cookies Decaffeinated coffee	1 Natural Bran Muffin 1 or more glasses of Water	Banana smoothie= 1/8 c. orange juice, 1 banana Water and ice cubes 1 Rice cake
Dinner	Roast Duck Wild Rice Stuffing Carrot sticks Sliced nectarine on a bed of lettuce with 6 raw cashews Water or selection from the beverage section.	Easy Fish (4-6 oz.) Onions and Mushrooms, stir-fry in soy sauce Baked Potato with 1 tsp. margarine Pepper Slaw Water or selection from the beverage section	Cuban Black Beans and Rice Cucumber Salad with Green Pepper in 1 tbsp. Safflower oil Unlimited vinegar and herbs 1/4 c. lightly cooked Carrots Water or selection from the beverage section.	2 Stuffed Chicken Legs Mushroom-Sprout Delight 1 Quick Corn Muffin Water or selection from the beverage section	3/4 -1 c. Vegetable Barley Mushroom Delight Soup 3-4 oz. Baked Red Snapper Steamed Corn on the cob Water or selection from the beverage section	Fish with Zucchini baked Yellow Squash medium baked Potato Water or selection from the beverage section.	Chicken Nani Steamed Brown Rice ½ c. Lima Beans Tomato slices with Mushroom slices and Vinaigrette dressing Water or selection from the beverage section
Snack	2-3 Banana Raisin Cookies Decaffeinated coffee	1 Natural Bran Muffin 1 or more glasses of Water	Banana smoothie = 1/8 c. orange juice, 1 banana Water and ice cubes 1 Rice cake	3/4 c. Fruit and Nut Snack Mix 1 or more glasses of Water	1 Banana 1 Rice cake 1 or more glasses of Water	1 Apple 6-8 raw Cashews 1 or more glasses of Water	1 slice Whole Grain Bread 1 tsp. raw Almond Butter 1 or more glasses of Water

Table 12

APPENDICES

APPENDIX 1

REVISED NATIONAL DIETARY GOALS

The main purpose of this book is to bring to you as a PMS woman, information that will allow you to contain your symptoms through what you eat or doesn't eat, that is, nutritional treatment of PMS symptoms. We would not feel that this book is complete without a discussion of what a "basic healthy diet" is all about. This section should be used along with he information in Section I to help you to create your own personal optimum diet. It is our belief that PMS is part of a much larger problem. This problem is *wellness,* how to get it and how to keep it. The foods we eat make a difference in how our body functions. We are already familiar with the fact that many *diseases* and medical conditions are related to nutrition, to what we eat and because of what we do not eat. PMS is the example at hand, but there are others conditions such as: heart disease, stroke, high blood pressure, diabetes, arthritis, fibrocystic disease of the breasts, intestinal diseases, stomach diseases, gall bladder disease and even in some cases, cancer.

What you have eaten in the past has caused you to get PMS. We believe through the approach presented in this work we can relieve, even *cure*, PMS. But what about your family, what will happen to them if their diet does not change? What should their diets be like? How can you help them?

In order to answer these questions we would have to write a whole new book. What we will do is provide you with the revised national guide lines as published in the Consumer Nutrition Institute Weekly Report Vol.8 (4):6, 1978. It fits closest with our particular philosophy and can be used as a model to help you to create your own guidelines for you and for your family.

1. To avoid becoming overweight, consume only as much energy (calories) as is expended; if overweight, decrease energy intake and increase energy expenditure. (See Appendix 8.)

2. Increase the consumption of complex carbohydrates and "naturally occurring" sugars from about 28% energy intake to about 48% (or greater) energy intake.

3. Reduce the consumption of refined and processed sugars by 45% (or more) to account for about (no more than) 10% of total energy intake. (See Appendix 7.)

4. Reduce overall fat consumption from approximately 40% to about (no more than) 30% of energy intake. (See Appendix 6.)

30 Days To No More PMS
The Cook Book

5. Reduce saturated fat consumption to account for about (no more than) 10% of total energy intake; and balance that with polyunsaturated and mono-saturated fats, which should account for about (no more than) 10% of energy intake each. (See Appendix 6.)

6. Reduce the intake of cholesterol to about (no more than) 300 mg. a day.

7. Limit the intake of sodium by reducing the intake of salt to about (no more than) 5 grams a day. (See Appendix 12.)

The goals suggest the following change in food selection and preparation:

1. Increase consumption of fruits and vegetables and whole grains.

2. Decrease consumption of refined and other processed sugars and foods high in such sugars.

3. Decrease consumption of foods high in total fats, and partially replace saturated fats, whether obtained from animal or vegetable sources, with polyunsaturated fats.

4. Decrease consumption of animal fat, and choose meats, poultry and fish which will reduce saturated fat intake.

5. Substitute low-fat milk for whole milk, and low-fat dairy products for high fat dairy products.

6. Decrease consumption of butter fat, eggs, and other high cholesterol sources. Some consideration should be given to easing the cholesterol goal for young children and the elderly in order to obtain the nutritional benefits of eggs in the diet.

7. Decrease consumption of salt and foods high in salt content.

You may notice that these guidelines are very similar to those we have suggested in the text of this book. These guidelines are general and may fit your family's needs but please note those differences that are suggested for the relief of the symptoms of PMS.

APPENDIX 2

FOODS HIGH IN MAGNESIUM

One of the most important aspects of the nutritional-dietary approach to PMS is the elimination of excess calcium and the supplementation of magnesium. Supplementation can be done by one of two methods 1) picking foods which are high in magnesium and low in calcium that is have high mg/Ca Ratio's, or 2) vitamin-mineral supplements. In some women both are necessary. In order to facilitate using the least supplements and getting the best results, we are providing you with two lists of foods, *Foods Very High in Magnesium* within this section and *Foods to Avoid-High in Calcium* in Appendix 3. You can use these lists to help you pick foods which are higher in magnesium and lowest in calcium. If you learn how to uses these lists you can reduce not only the amount of supplements you might need to take, but also the severity of your PMS symptoms.

In order to help you pick foods that will decrease your PMS, we have listed the foods by their Magnesium to Calcium Ratio. That is, Mg/Ca ratios since, as we suggested earlier, it is most important that your intake of magnesium must be at least 2 Mg to every 1 Ca you eat. Since calcium *is* necessary for your overall well-being, we would not wish for you to eliminate it entirely, even if you could, which you can't. At best what you can decrease calcium and increase magnesium intake. On the *Foods Very High in Magnesium* list we have placed the foods in decreasing order from foods with the highest Mg\Ca ratio down to those with the lowest Mg/Ca ratio. The absolute amounts of calcium and magnesium are also important and must be watched if symptoms are a problem. It is important to note that using the Mg/Ca ration allows you to not have to be concerned about how much of any individual food you will eat. That is the Mg/Ca ratio is the same if you eat one ounce of a specific food or one pound of this same food. True the total amount of magnesium you will get will increase, but it is also true that the total amount of calcium you get will be equally as large. Hence the real value is that you can pick your food s to eat and not have to worry about the portions, weighting them or what will happen as you cook or combine them, as everything will stay the same.

HOW TO USE THE DESIRED FOODS AND FOODS TO BE AVOIDED LISTS

The magnesium and calcium contents of the foods listed above, are in milligrams (mg.) per serving size of each food listed. The Mg/Ca ratios are calculated by dividing the amount of magnesium in milligrams (mg.) by the amount of calcium in milligrams (mg.). The number produced now indicates the relative proportion of magnesium to calcium. Thus as with Sweet corn unit of the corn contains 48 mg. of magnesium and 3 mg. of calcium.

30 Days To No More PMS
The Cook Book

Thus:

   48.0 mg. of magnesium divided by 3.0 mg. of calcium = 16
   or 16 times more magnesium then calcium.

   48 / 3 = 16.0

   Therefore there are 16 mg. of magnesium to each 1 mg. of calcium no matter the serving size.

   Therefore, no matter how much corn you eat there will always be 16 times more magnesium than calcium.

Another way of saying this is that for Sweet corn the Mg/Ca ratio, the ratio of magnesium to calcium is:

   16 to 1

   This can also be abbreviated both as:

   16:1 and as 16/1

Another example of determining the ratio of magnesium to calcium is:

Cashews have 267 mg. of magnesium and 38 mg. of calcium, therefore:

   267 / 38 = 6.8
   here we have calculated to only one decimal point, we could have rounded the number off to 7.0 but we chose to be just a little more accurate then convenient.

For each of the foods listed the Mg/Ca number below represents the ratio of magnesium to calcium. We can also use 16.0:1 or 3.8:1 or shorten it simply to 16.0 or 3.8 as they all mean exactly the same thing.

30 Days To No More PMS
The Cook Book

DESIRED FOODS
HIGH MAGNESIUM FOODS
FOODS TO BE EATEN AS OFTEN AS POSSIBLE

FOODS WITH HIGH MG/CA RATIO	MG	CA	MG/CA
FRUITS			
Banana, raw, 1 medium	33	7	4.7
Banana, dried, 1 oz.	132	32	4.1
Passion fruit (Purple Grandilla), raw 1 medium	5	2	2.5
FRUIT & VEGETABLE JUICES			
Passion fruit, yellow, fresh, 8 fl. oz.	41	9	4.6
Coconut, milk, canned, 1 cup	104	40	2.6
Coconut, milk, raw, 1 cup	89	39	2.3
VEGETABLES			
Mushrooms, shiitake, dried, 4	20	2	10.0
Avocado, Florida, 1 medium	104	33	5.5
Mushrooms, shiitake, cooked, 4	10	2	5.0
Potato, baked without skin, 1 medium	39	8	4.9
Potato, microwaved without skin, 1 medium	39	8	4.9
Avocado, California, 1 medium	70	19	3.7
Beets, boiled, ½ cup	31	9	3.4
Succotash, cooked, ½ cup	51	16	3.2
Black-eyed peas (cow peas), dried, raw, ½ cup	230	75	3.1
Peas, green, dried, ½ cup	180	64	2.8
Peas, green, split, cooked 1 cup	31	22	2.7
Potato, baked with skin, 1 medium	55	20	2.75
Potato, hash browns, homemade, 1 medium	16	6	2.7
Black beans, cooked, 1 cup	121	47	2.6
Lima beans, cooked or dried, 1 cup	82	32	2.6
Potato, boiled without skin, 1 medium	26	10	2.6
Sesame, kernel, toasted 1 Tablespoon	98	37	2.6
Ginger root, raw, ½ cup sliced	10	4	2.5
Mushrooms, cooked, ½ cup	10	4	2.5
Potato, microwaved with skin, 1 medium	54	22	2.45
Dock, raw or cooked, ½ cup	69	29	2.4
Pepper, sweet, raw or cooked ½ cup	7	3	2.3
Cowpeas (Black-eyed peas), cooked, ½ cup	91	42	2.2
GRAINS, BREADS, PASTAS & CRACKERS			
Corn germ, Ener G Foods, 1 cup	672	Trace	672:1
Sweet corn, 1 ear	48	3	16.0
Corn meal, Quaker Enriched./Aunt Jemima, 1 cup	12	Trace	12.0

30 Days To No More PMS
The Cook Book

FOODS WITH HIGH MG/CA RATIO	MG	CA	MG/CA
Millet, 3.5 oz.	162	20	8.1
Wheat bran, Quaker unprocessed, 2 Tablespoon	46	6	7.7
Wheat germ, toasted, ¼ cup (1 oz.)	91	13	7.0
Rice, wild, ½ cup	129	19	7.0
Rice flour, Ener G Foods, ½ cup	60	13	4.6
Wheat, whole grain, 1 cup	160	40	4.0
Oat bran, Quaker, 1/3 cup (1 oz.)	67	20	3.4
Barley, Scotch, 1 cup	34	11	3.1
Rye grain, whole, 1 cup	115	38	3.0
Oats, oatmeal, quick, 1/3 cup dry (2/3 cooked)	40	14	2.9
Brown rice, ½ cup	88	32	2.8
Rye Krisp Crackers, plain and seasoned, ¼ sq.	34	12	2.8
Macaroni, enriched, cooked (not cheese) 1 cup	25	11	2.3
Spaghetti, enriched, cooked, 1 cup	25	11	2.3
Barley, light pearl, 1 cup	37	16	2.3
Buckwheat, whole grain, 1 cup	229	114	2.0

NUTS & SEEDS (All 1 ounce servings)			
Pinyon, pine nuts, dried	67	2	33.5
Pumpkin seeds	152	12	12.7
Watermelon seeds	146	15	9.7
Ginko nuts, raw	8	1	8.0
Cashew butter	73	12	6.1
Cashews, dry roasted	74	13	5.7
Cashews, raw	74	13	5.7
Peanut butter, smooth/creamy	28	5	5.6
Chestnuts, roasted	26	5	5.2
Ginko nuts, canned	5	1	5.0
Chestnuts, dried	39	8	4.9
Butter nuts, dried	67	15	4.5
Acorns, Raw	5	24	4.8
Water chestnuts, Chinese	39	8	4.8
Pecans, dry roasted	10	38	3.8
Pecans, dry roasted	38	10	3.8
Coconut meat, dried	26	7	3.7
Peanuts, dry roasted	206	59	3.5
Sunflower seeds, dried	100	33	3.3
Sesame kernels, toasted	98	37	2.6
Coconut meat, fresh	14	6	2.3

For additional food values go to http://www.well-net.com/PMS/MG-CA-Lists/index.html.html

APPENDIX 3

FOODS TO AVOID - FOODS HIGH IN CALCIUM

This section will deal with what foods which are best avoided. The foods on this list are divided into two parts 1) foods to be *entirely avoided* 2) foods which can be considered *neutral*. The foods in the first section of this appendix are *Foods with Low Mg/Ca Ratios* hence must either be avoided entirely all month long in the woman with severe PMS symptoms or may be avoided primarily only during the critical period, the two weeks prior to the onset of your menstrual period, in women with milder PMS symptoms. The foods in the F*oods To Be Avoided List* are ones which will promote your PMS and make your symptoms worse. They are high in calcium and relatively low in magnesium. These foods have ratios less than 1.0. The foods in the second section, considered to be *Neutral Foods*, have just about equal amounts of calcium and magnesium. They should be avoided if you can choose a food(s) from Appendix 2, *Foods High in Magnesium*, but they are much better than the higher calcium foods. The foods in this second section, the Neutral Foods have magnesium to calcium ratios between 1.0 and 2.0.

These Foods to Avoid High Calcium list is ordered from the least desirable foods towards the most desirable foods, that is, the lowest Mg/Ca ratio to the highest Mg/Ca ratio, while the Neutral Foods list is ordered from the best food (highest in magnesium) to the worst (highest in calcium).

HOW TO USE THE FOODS TO AVOID (HIGH CALCIUM) LIST

This list is used very much like the list in Appendix 2, the Mg/Ca ratios are calculated exactly the same way. However, in this list we have placed the calcium values first, this is only to allow you to visualize the relative amounts of calcium to magnesium.

Similarly to the list in Appendix 2, the numbers on the far right of this list represent the ratio of magnesium to calcium (Mg/Ca). These numbers may be represented, for example as, Endive 0.12:1 or 0.12 units of magnesium to every 1 unit of calcium. Another way to say this is that for 1 mg. of calcium there are 0.12 mg. of magnesium. You can now see that the foods on this list have much more calcium then magnesium and therefore, should be avoided. The smaller the number the more calcium (also the less magnesium). As the numbers increase the relative amounts of magnesium increase and the foods become less of a problem to the calcium sensitive woman.

The reader should take note as to how many more "high" calcium foods there are when compared

30 Days To No More PMS
The Cook Book

to "high" magnesium foods. It may once again allow you to see why PMS is such a common problem in our society. Each woman might also make a list of the 10 most common foods she eats and note they are most likely foods which are significantly higher in Calcium than Magnesium. If you do this for yourself we believe that you will certainly be able to see why you have PMS. (See the Forms Section for a form to use to do this.)

The values for magnesium and calcium on these lists come from a number of different sources. Where there might be considerable disagreement between sources both values are listed. The values are not averaged although most are rounded off to the first decimal point. The values are to be used as a general figure and are provided simply to present an overall sense of the Mg/Ca ratios of a wide variety of foods. Most of the foods we will present to you will be considerably higher in Ca than Mg.

FOODS TO AVOID
HIGH CALCIUM FOODS

FOODS WITH LOW MG/CA RATIOS	CA	MG	MG/CA
FRUITS			
Kumquats, raw, 1 medium	31	.31	0.01
Orange, Valencia, 1 medium	48	12	0.25
Orange, Naval, 1 medium	56	15	0.26
Crabapple, raw, 1 cup slices	20	7	0.35
Currants, red and white, raw, ½ cup	18	7	0.40
Gooseberry, raw, 1 cup	38	15	0.40
Grapes, American, raw, 1 cup	13	5	0.40
Papaya, raw, 1 medium	72	31	0.40
Fig, raw, 1 medium	18	8	0.40
Fig, dried, 10	269	111	0.40
Currants, black, European, raw, ½ cup	31	14	0.45
Mulberries, raw, 1 cup	55	25	0.45
Pear, fresh, 1 medium	19	9	0.47
Grapes, European, raw, 1 cup	17	10	0.47
Apricot, fresh, 3 medium	15	8	0.50
Guava, raw, 1 medium	18	9	0.50
Cherry, red sour, canned, water pack, ½ cup	13	7	0.54
Boysenberries, frozen, 1 cup, unsweetened	36	21	0.58
Apple, whole with skin medium	10	6	0.60
Blackberries, raw, ½ cup	23	14	0.60
Cranberries, raw, 1 cup, whole	7	5	0.70
Quince, raw, 1 medium	10	7	0.70
Raisins, seedless, 2/3 cup	49	33	0.70

30 Days To No More PMS
The Cook Book

FOODS WITH HIGH MG/CA RATIO	MG	CA	MG/CA
Apple, pared, 1 medium	6	5	0.80
Blueberries, raw, ½ cup	9	7	0.80
Cherries, raw, 10	10	8	0.80
Guava, Strawberry, raw, 1 cup	52	14	0.80
Grapefruit, pink, red and white, ½ medium	13	10	0.80
Loganberry, frozen, 1 cup	38	32	0.80
Loquats, raw, 10 medium	16	13	0.80
Raspberries, red, raw, 10	27	22	0.80
Strawberries, raw, 1 cup	21	16	0.80
Tangerine, raw, 1 medium	12	10	0.80
Prunes, cooked, ½ cup	24	21	0.87
Apple, dried, 10 rings	9	10	0.90
Mango, raw, 1 medium	21	18	0.90
Oheloberries, raw, 1 cup	10	9	0.90
Prune, dried, 10	43	38	0.90
Pear, dried, 10 halves	59	58	0.98

FRUIT & VEGETABLE JUICES			
Papaya, nectar, canned, 8 fl. oz.	24	8	0.33
Pear, nectar, canned, fl. oz.	11	6	0.54
Carrot, canned, 6 fl. oz.	44	26	0.60
Pineapple, canned and frozen, 8 fl. oz.	42	34	0.80
Peach, nectar, canned, 8 fl. oz.	13	11	0.85
Apple, frozen, concentrate, hydrated, 8 fl. oz.	14	12	0.86
Lemon, fresh, 8 fl. oz.	18	16	0.90

VEGETABLES			
Rhubarb, frozen, cooked, sweetened, 1 cup	174	15	0.08
Cabbage, Chinese, cooked, ½ cup	79	9	0.11
Garlic, raw, 3 cloves	16	2	0.13
Kale leaves, frozen, ½ cup chopped	90	12	0.13
Mustard greens, frozen, ½ cup chopped	75	10	0.13
Cress, Garden, 5-8 sprigs	81	11	0.14
Collard greens, frozen, ½ cup	179	26	0.15
Dandelion greens, raw, ½ cup chopped	52	10	0.20
Cabbage, Chinese, raw, ½ cup shredded	39	9	0.20
Watercress, raw, ½ cup chopped	20	4	0.20
Lettuce, Romaine, raw, ½ cup shredded	10	2	0.20
Turnip greens, cooked, ½ cup	125	21	0.20
Horseradish, 1 Tablespoon	28	7	0.25
Cabbage, green, raw, ½ cup shredded	16	5	0.30
Cabbage, red, raw, ½ cup shredded	18	5	0.30
Celery, raw or cooked, 1 stalk (7.5 inches long)	15	5	0.30
Chicory, greens, raw, ½ cup chopped	90	27	0.30
Endive (escarole), raw, ½ cup chopped	13	4	0.30
Parsley, raw, ½ cup chopped	39	13	0.30
Olives, green pickled, 2 medium	61	22	0.40

30 Days To No More PMS
The Cook Book

FOODS WITH HIGH MG/CA RATIO	MG	CA	MG/CA
Onion, raw, cooked or dried, ½ cup chopped	20	08	0.40
Broccoli, cooked, frozen, ½ cup	47	19	0.40
Cauliflower, cooked, ½ cup	17	7	0.40
Sesame seeds, toasted and roasted, 1 oz.	281	101	0.40
Cabbage, cooked, ½ cup shredded	25	11	0.44
Turnip, ½ cup cubes	32	14	0.44
Broccoli, raw, ½ cup pieces	89	11	0.50
Cauliflower, raw, ½ cup pieces	14	7	0.50
Leek, raw, ¼ cup chopped	15	7	0.50
Lettuce, iceberg, 1 leaf	4	2	0.50
Rutabaga, cooked, ½ cup	36	18	0.50
Spinach, cooked, frozen, ½ cup	139	65	0.50
Tofu, firm, raw, ½ cup	258	118	0.50
Brussels sprouts, cooked, ½ cup (4 sprouts)	28	16	0.60
Carrots, cooked, ½ cup sliced	19	11	0.60
Carrots, raw, 1 medium	19	11	0.60
Pumpkin, cooked, ½ cup mashed	18	11	0.60
Snap beans, green/yellow, cooked, ½ cup	29	16	0.60
Squash, winter, baked, ½ cup cubed	14	8	0.60
Spinach, New Zealand, frozen, cooked, ½ cup	43	29	0.70
Sweet potato, baked, 1 medium	32	23	0.70
Kelp, 3.5 oz.	168	121	0.70
Dulse, ½ cup	296	220	0.70
Kidney, red California beans, cooked, 1 cup	116	85	0.70
Potato, homemade mashed, ½ cup	27	19	0.70
Navy beans, cooked, 1 cup	128	107	0.80
Parsnip, cooked, ½ cup	29	23	0.80
Spinach, raw, ½ cup chopped	28	22	0.80
Asparagus, cooked, ½ cup (6 spears)	22	17	0.90
Alfalfa seed sprouts, raw, 1 cup	10	9	0.90
Chick peas (garbanzo beans), canned, 1 cup	78	70	0.90
Cucumber, raw, ½ cup sliced	7	6	0.90
French beans, cooked, 1 cup	111	99	0.90
Green peas, canned, ½ cup	17	15	0.90
Okra, cooked, ½ cup	50	46	0.90
Squash, summer, cooked, ½ cup sliced	24	22	0.90
GRAIN, BREAD & CRACKERS			
Hamburger buns, 1 roll	54	8	0.15
Hot dog buns, 1 roll	54	8	0.15
White bread, 1 slice	30	5	0.16
French bread, 1 slice	22	6	0.27
Pita bread, pita	31	10	0.30
Rye bread, American, 1 slice	20	6	0.30
Wheat bread, 1 slice	30	11	0.40
Bagels, 1 bagel	25	11	0.44
Saltine crackers, 2 crackers	4	2	0.50

30 Days To No More PMS
The Cook Book

FOODS WITH HIGH MG/CA RATIO	MG	CA	MG/CA
Corn tortilla, 1 tortilla	42	20	0.50
Taco/tostada shell, 1 shell	16	11	0.70
NUTS & SEEDS (All 1 ounce servings)			
Walnuts, black	15	57	0.30
Mixed Nuts, dry roasted	20	64	0.30
Sesame, whole, roasted/toasted	281	101	0.40
Brazil Nuts, dried	64	50	0.80
Soy nuts, dry roasted, ½ cup	232	196	0.84
Filberts	209	184	0.90

For additional food values go to http://www.well-net.com/PMS/MG-CA-Lists/index.html

FOODS WHICH ARE BASICALLY NEUTRAL

FOODS WITH LOW MG/CA RATIOS	CA	MG	MG/CA
FRUITS			
Applesauce, unsweetened, ½ cup	4	4	1.00
Apricot, dried, 10 halves	16	16	1.00
Dates, dried, 10	27	29	1.00
Pear, canned, water pack, 1 cup	9	9	1.00
Raspberries, Black, raw, 2/3 cup	30	30	1.00
Cantaloupe, 1 cup pieces	17	17	1.00
Jackfruit, raw, 3.5 oz	34	37	1.00
Kiwi, raw, 1 medium	20	23	1.15
Peach, fresh, 1 medium	5	6	1.20
Peach. canned, water pack 1 cup	15	18	1.20
Persimmon, Japanese, raw, 1 cup pieces	13	15	1.20
Tamarind, raw, 1 cup	89	110	1.24
Lychees, dried, 3.5 oz	33	42	1.30
Watermelon, raw, 1 cup pieces	13	17	1.30
Melon balls (cantaloupe/honeydew), frozen, 1 cup	17	24	1.40
Breadfruit, raw, 1 medium	17	24	1.40
Acerola, raw, 1 cup	12	18	1.50
Carissa, raw, 1 medium	2	3	1.50
Peach, dried, 10 halves	37	54	1.50
Prickly pear, raw, 1 medium	58	88	1.50
Casaba melon, raw, 1 cup, pieces	9	14	1.60
Nectarine, raw, 1 medium	6	11	1.80
Pineapple, raw, 1 cup, pieces	11	21	1.90
Carambola, raw, 1 medium	6	12	2.00
Lychees, raw, 10	5	10	2.00
Plum, raw, 1 medium	2	4	2.00

30 Days To No More PMS
The Cook Book

FOODS WITH HIGH MG/CA RATIO	MG	CA	MG/CA
FRUIT & VEGETABLE JUICES			
Coconut water	58	60	1.00
Orange, fresh, 8 fl. oz.	27	27	1.00
Vegetable Cocktail, 6 fl. oz.	20	20	1.00
Acerola, 8 fl. oz.	24	29	1.20
Prune, canned, 8 fl. oz.	30	36	1.20
Tomato, fresh, 6 fl. oz.	16	22	1.25
Orange, canned, 8 fl. oz.	21	27	1.30
Grapefruit, canned, 8 fl. oz.	18	26	1.30
Grapefruit, fresh, 8 fl. oz.	22	30	1.36
VEGETABLES			
Artichoke, Jerusalem, cooked, 1 medium	47	47	1.00
Chick peas (garbanzo beans), cooked, 1 cup	80	78	1.00
Chive, 1 Tablespoon	2	2	1.00
Brussels sprouts, frozen, ½ cup	19	19	1.00
Mixed vegetables, frozen, ½ cup	22	20	1.00
Tofu, raw, ½ cup	130	127	1.00
Pigeon pea, cooked, 1 cup	72	77	1.10
Soybean, dried, ½ cup	226	265	1.20
Squash, summer, raw, ½ cup	13	15	1.20
White beans, dried, 1 cup	144	170	1.20
Pinto beans cooked, 1 cup	82	95	1.20
Yellow beans, cooked, 1 cup	110	131	1.20
Pink beans, cooked, 1 cup	88	110	1.25
Eggplant, broiled, ½ cup	12	16	1.30
Yams, baked, ½ cup cubed	9	12	1.30
Green peas, fresh or cooked, ½ cup	22	31	1.40
Cow Peas (Black-eyed), cooked, 1 cup	48	66	1.40
Kidney red beans, cooked,	50	80	1.40
Poi, cooked, ½ cup	19	29	1.50
Red beans, dried, ½ cup	110	163	1.50
Swiss chard, ½ cup chopped	51	76	1.50
Zucchini, raw, ½ cup sliced	19	29	1.50
Mung beans sprouted, raw, ½ cup	7	11	1.60
Zucchini, cooked, ½ cup sliced	12	19	1.60
Taro, cooked, ½ cup sliced	12	20	1.66
Succotash, canned or frozen, ½ cup	14	24	1.70
Tomato, raw or cooked, 1 tomato	8	14	1.75
Adzuki beans, cooked, 1 cup	63	120	1.90
Lentils, boiled, 1 cup	71	37	1.90
Lima beans, baby, cooked, 1 cup	52	97	1.90
GRAINS, BREADS, PASTAS & CRACKERS			
Pumpernickel Bread, toasted, 1 slice	23	22	1.00
Rice, White, 1 cup	24	28	1.20
Soy Bean, low fat, ½ cup	165	202	1.20

30 Days To No More PMS
The Cook Book

FOODS WITH HIGH MG/CA RATIO	MG	CA	MG/CA
Soy Bean, defatted, ½ cup	297	373	1.25
Whole Wheat Bread, 1 slice	18	23	1.30
French Rolls, Enriched, 1 roll	8	12	1.50
Noodles, Enriched, Cooked, 1 cup	16	28	1.75
NUTS & SEEDS (All 1 Ounce servings)			
Almonds, dry roasted	84	84	1.00
Pistachio nuts, dried (47 nuts)	38	45	1.20
Chestnuts, Chinese, raw	27	41	1.50
Hazelnuts, dried/roasted	55	84	1.50
Macadamia Nuts, dried	20	33	1.70
Walnuts, English	27	48	1.80
Sunflower Seeds, dry roasted	20	37	1.85

MEATS

Game meats tend to have higher Mg/Ca ratios. Larger muscles generally mean more magnesium. Some cuts of beef can be as high as 9.2. Pork loin can be as high as 7.6, lamb 5.7. In all meats the Mg/Ca ratio will ultimately not depend on which type of meat you chose but rather on the specific cut of the meat. Shoulder and roast seem generally higher. The flank area tends to run 4.0; ground beef, 2.4 to 3.0; top round, 5.2 and round tip 5.4. T-bone steaks can range form 1.7- 4.1.

Chicken tends to be in the area of 2 to 1 ratio Mg/Ca depending on the specific parts. White meats tend to be higher in magnesium while dark meats are lower. Duck ranges from 1.5 to 1.8. Turkey averages 2.5 to 1 Mg/Ca. Game poultry appears to have higher mg/Ca values than form raised poultry. Smoked turkey is higher in magnesium but smoked meats often contain sugar so they may not be a good choice for sensitive women. We suggest staying away from luncheon meats because, with the exception of turkey breast meats, they are generally higher in calcium. All ratios depend on mode of cooking. Roasting meats tends to help retain higher ratios when compared to frying meats.

SEA FOODS

Deep sea fish such as chard, swordfish, Walleye, Atlantic cod, Sockeye and red salmon, flounder, Pacific cod, Scrod, sturgeon, scallops are all over 2.0 along with a host of other fish types.

NON-MEAT PROTEINS

On top of the list is peanut butter but also pumpkin and squash seeds, cashews and cashew butter, sunflower seeds and butter, pistachios and Lentil wafers are all greater than 2.0

30 Days To No More PMS
The Cook Book

For additional Meat, Sea Foods, Non-Meat Protein Source values go to http://www.well-net.com/PMS/MG-CA-Lists/index.html

DRINKS

Since water, unless it is distilled, is generally high in calcium, most drinks will also be higher in calcium. Of course, drinks made with dairy products, yogurt, milk, such as malts, milk shakes and smoothies will be high in calcium as well.

We recommend not worrying about the Ca/Mg ratio of your drinks and we suggest that you just use water and other fluids (except those made with dairy products) as much as you want and need as they are essential to your overall health. We generally recommend that every woman drink at least 8 to 10 eight-ounce glasses of water or other fluids each day. While we suggest you do not drink caffeinated drinks (i.e., coffee and teas, etc.), you can drink decaffeinated coffee in moderation (as it still has some caffeine) and caffeine free herbal teas as much as you desire.

Please read labels on soft drinks to avoid caffeinated products and of course avoid all products with chocolate whether caffeine is listed or not. Most foods and drinks which include chocolate *do not list the caffeine within it.*

APPENDIX 4

CAFFEINE CONTENT OF FOODS

We have previously discussed the relationship of caffeine to PMS. This table lists the caffeine content of those foods and beverages which contain caffeine. Caffeine content will be given in mg/serving. The actual amounts of caffeine will vary based on processing and variations in beans, leaves and length of brewing, strength of the portions, etc. Generally a standard cup 6 oz cup is used as the serving size, therefore, if for example a regular 6 fl oz cup of coffee were to have 103 mg of caffeine within it, if you were to drink 3 cups of this coffee each day you would be getting 3 x 103 or 309 mgs of caffeine daily.

An 8 fl oz cup of coffee would contain 33% more caffeine than a 6 fl oz cup. A 12 oz mug would contain twice as much caffeine and so on. This should give the reader some sense of how to evaluate how much caffeine you are actually ingesting on a daily basis. Remember, in other than the most severe situations, most PMS women need only pay attention to caffeine intake during the critical phase of the cycle, the last two weeks prior to the onset of their menstruation, usually starting 2 to 3 days before your PMS symptoms begin.

Once again these values we are presenting here may vary so it is important to read labels to determine if caffeine is in a specific product and if necessary how much.

FOOD   **MG CAFFEINE/SERVING**

COFFEE BEVERAGES:
brewed, ground	103/cup (range 85-200/cup)
percolated	110/cup (range 97-125/cup)
dripolated	146/cup (range 137-153/cup)
instant	60/rd t
instant, decaffeinated	2/rd t

TEA BEVERAGES (HOT OR ICED, BREWED 5 MIN.):
regular, bagged	46/cup
regular, loose	40/cup
Oolong, bagged	40/cup
green, loose	35/cup
green, bagged	31/cup
instant - 1 rd t	31/cup
Darjeeling, loose	28/cup

30 Days To No More PMS
The Cook Book

FOOD	MG CAFFEINE/SERVING
Oolong, loose	24/cup
Japanese green, loose	20/cup

COCOA AND COLA BEVERAGES:

cocoa/hot chocolate beverages	13/cup (range 6-42/cup)
cola beverage	47/12 oz. (range 30-90/12 oz.)

SPECIFIC BRANDS:

COFFEE, INSTANT DRY POWDER

Hills Brothers	189/cup
Maxim, freeze-dried	61/tsp
Nescafe, Nestle	59/tsp
Tasters Choice, Nestle	59/tsp
Mellow Roast	56/tsp
Yuban	56/tsp
Orange Cappuccino	33/tsp
Café Vienna	31/tsp
Café Francais	30/tsp
Suisse Mocha	29/tsp
Brim, freeze-dried, decaffeinated	3/tsp
Tasters Choice, decaffeinated	5/tsp
Sanka	3/tsp
Sanka, Freeze-dried	3/tsp

TEA BEVERAGE (HOT OR ICED):

Tender Leaf	66/cup
MJB	62/cup
Twinnings English	61/cup
Canterbury	54/cup
Lipton, bagged	54/cup
Lipton, loose	51/cup
Swee-Touch-Nee	47/cup

30 Days To No More PMS
The Cook Book

FOOD	MG CAFFEINE/SERVING
Harvest Day	4 /cup 5
Pantry Pride	45/cup
Nestle, instant iced/lemon	42/cup
Bigelow Constant Comment	31/cup
Boston's 99 ½% caffeine-free	9/cup

CHOCOLATE BEVERAGE DRY MIX:

cocoa, mix, instant Carnation	13/pkg
choc powder, instant dry, Hershey	10/tbsp
cocoa, dry, Hershey	10 tbsp
cocoa, instant, Hershey	10/tbsp
cocoa, mix , instant	9/tbsp

CHOCOLATE BEVERAGE:

cocoa mix (water) Carnation	14/cup

CARBONATED BEVERAGES:

Dr. Pepper	61/12 oz.
Mountain Dew	55/12 oz.
Dr. Pepper sugar free	54/12 oz.
Mello Yellow	52/12 oz.
Cherry Cola Slice	48/12 oz.
Pepsi Cola sugar free	48/12 oz.
Cocoa Cola	46/12 oz.
Tab sugar free	46/12 oz.
Mr. Pibb	40/12 oz.
Pepsi Cola	38/12 oz.
Pepsi Light	36/12 oz.
Diet Rite Cola	33/12 oz.
Royal Crown Cola	34/12 oz.
Royal Crown Cola sugar free	33/12 oz.
Royal Crown w/a Twist	21/12 oz.

30 Days To No More PMS
The Cook Book

FOOD   **MG CAFFEINE/SERVING**

SPECIFIC BRAND PRODUCTS:

General Foods International Coffees	25-73 /6 fl oz cup
Many Jell-O Choc food products contain caffeine	4-12 /½ cup
No Doz, Vivarin	100-200/pill
Excedrin, Anacin	60/pill
Pre-Mens	66/pill
Aspirin compound-phenacetin-caffeine	32/pill
Cope, Midol, etc.	32/pill
Dristan, Sinarest	30/pill

APPENDIX 5

FOOD ADDITIVES IN YOUR FOOD

The following list of food additives represents only a small portion of some 2,116 commonly used food additives, colorings, food dyes, preservatives etc. for the great majority of these food additives, their exact effects on the human body and their metabolic processes are still not clearly understood or known. The ultimate short and long term effects of these chemicals are also unknown. It is our position that they should be avoided as much as is possible. We feel that many may worsen PMS by causing shortages of necessary vitamins and minerals, especially Vitamin B6 and magnesium. Some are primary sources of calcium in themselves and even though found in small amounts, may worsen symptoms of calcium sensitive women.

FOOD ADDITIVES	**COMMENTS, USES AND POSSIBLE PHYSIOLOGICAL EFFECTS**
MULTIPURPOSE	
Aluminum ammonium sulfate	May lead to increased aluminum ingestion, which has been suggested to have possible adverse effects on brain function.
Aluminum potassium sulfate	
Aluminum sodium sulfate	
Aluminum sulfate	
Caffeine	Increased adrenalin activity, possible cancer or birth defects problems, elevated blood pressure, hair loss in males. Worsens PMS, fibrocystic breast disease. Habit forming, causes headaches and insomnia.
Citric acid	Has produced allergic reactions in some individuals.
Ethyl formate	Petrochemical products of possible toxicity in excessive amounts.
Glyceryl monostearate	A fatty derivative used for texturing.
Lecithin	A complex natural fat used for emulsifying fats with water.
Methyl cellulose	A bulking agent of no nutritive value.
Monosodium glutamate	An amino acid derivative used as a flavor enhancer, It has produced the "Chinese restaurant syndrome" of abdominal cramping, nausea and headaches. It is also an unnecessary source of sodium.
Potassium bicarbonate	An alkalizing substance, which is found in baked goods.
Propylene glycol	A fat-like substance similar to antifreeze, which is found in ice milks.
Sodium carboxymethyl	A bulking agent of no nutritive cellulose value.

30 Days To No More PMS
The Cook Book

FOOD ADDITIVES	COMMENTS, USES AND POSSIBLE PHYSIOLOGICAL EFFECTS
Sodium tripolyphosphate	A source of both phosphorus and sodium, both of which may already be excessive in the diet. Found in soft drinks. All additives with sodium in the name contribute to elevated blood pressure and kidney problems.

ANTICAKING AGENTS:

Aluminum calcium silicate, sodium aluminoscilicate, sodium calcium aluminoscilicate	All sources of dietary aluminum, see information on aluminum above. Can be extra source of Calcium.

PRESERVATIVES:

Ascorbic acid	Vitamin C as it is commonly known.
Butylated hydroxyanisol (BHA)	Antioxidants which have been
Butylated hydroxytoluene (BHT)	shown to cause potential lung changes and hypersensitivity.
Calcium ascorbate, sodium ascorbate	Forms of Vitamin C. Extra source of both calcium and sodium.
Dilauryl thiodipropionate, erythorbic acid	Mold growth preventives
Potassium bisulfide, potassium metabisulfite, sodium metabisulfite	Found to cause genetic changes in some animals.
Stannous chloride	A source of tin which may be toxic at high levels.
Sodium and potassium EDTA, calcium disodium EDTA	Prevents minerals in foods from being available. Extra source of calcium.
Sodium nitrite	Used in smoked meats and hot dogs, ham, bacon, and sausage, this preservative may encourage formation of the cancer-causing substances nitrosamines.

EMULSIFYING AGENTS:

Cholic acid, desoxycholic acid, ox-bile extract	A bile acid derivative, which can prevent bile formation.
Mono- and di-glycerides	Form of animal or vegetable fat.

30 Days To No More PMS
The Cook Book

FOOD ADDITIVES	COMMENTS, USES AND POSSIBLE PHYSIOLOGICAL EFFECTS

PETROCHEMICAL-DERIVED COATINGS:
Coumarone-indere resin
Morpholine
Oxidized polyccylamine
Terpene resin
Synthetic paraffin
Petroleum naphtha

FLAVORINGS AND RELATED ENHANCERS:
Disodium guanylate
Disodium inosinate
Dioctyl sodium sulfoccinate

GUMS AND BASES
Polysorbate 80
Carrageenan
Arabinogalactan
Furcelleran

MULTIPURPOSE ADDITIVES

Acetone peroxide, azodicarbonamide	May induce tissue damage and aging.
Calcium steroyl-2-lactylate	Testing not adequate to define its potential toxicological effects.
Sodium lauryl sulfate, sodium stearoyl-2-lactylate, sodium stearoyl fumarate	Derivative of fats which are used in milk substitutes.
Gum tragacant	It has been shown to produce allergic reactions related to the "Big Mac Attack" of difficult breathing and shortness of breath. It is found in the "secret-sauce" of many hamburger relishes.
Sorbitol	A sugar derivative, which is not metabolized as readily as table sugar.

30 Days To No More PMS
The Cook Book

Benzoic acid, sodium benzoate   Metabolized in the liver and excreted.

Foods NOT on the FDA Generally Recognized as Safe (GRAS) List, may be approved under special conditions.

APPENDIX 6

LOW FAT EATING

In Appendix 1 Nutritional Guidelines we listed a number of suggestions regarding decreasing not only fats in your diet but decreasing *saturated fats* and relatively replacing them with *polyunsaturated fats*. Two questions may immediately come to your mind: How do I reduce fats? and How do I know saturated from polyunsaturated fats?

HOW TO REDUCE FATS FROM YOUR DIET?

1. Eat fish most often for animal protein.

2. Eat more turkey and chicken -- removing skin before cooking.

3. Eat less red meats -- beef, veal, pork, lamb.

4. Eliminate hot dogs, breaded fish, delicatessen meats (cold cuts, corned beef, pastrami, etc.) and restaurant hamburgers and other processed or preprepared meats.

5. Eliminate fried foods at home and when eating out.

6. Learn to cook without fats or oils -- bake, broil, steam, poach, BBQ.

7. Use no more than 1 tsp. of butter a day, no margarine, unless it is a polyunsaturated margarine.

8. Use nonfat milk and buttermilk -- no whole milk, no low-fat milk, no cream, no whipped cream, no sour cream, no cream cheese.

9. Use hoop cheese (skim milk cheese with no added salt).

10. For slicing and melting cheese use part skim milk cheese (string, mozzarella, etc.). One ounce twice a week only. During the premenstrual period it may be necessary to eliminate all cheeses entirely.

11. Use plain low fat yogurt in place of sour cream (on baked potato, for example) or Home Made Oil Mayonnaise type salad dressing. Two tablespoons a day only.

12. Nuts and seeds contain a large percentage of fats. They should be eaten fresh and raw only. One ounce a day at most.

13. Salad dressings are loaded with oil -- learn to use lemon juice or vinegar. Make your own at home.

14. Avoid restaurant foods cooked in fats and no butter on pop corn.

30 Days To No More PMS
The Cook Book

WHAT ARE THE SOURCES OF SATURATED AND UNSATURATED FATS?

SATURATED (Avoid)	**UNSATURATED** (Choose when possible.)
Whole milk	Corn oil, such as Mazola
Cream	Cottonseed oil, such as Wesson oil
Butter	Olives and olive oil
Ice cream	Safflower oil
Cheese (except cottage)	Sunflower oil
Beef	Soybean oil
Pork	Peanut oil or other vegetable oils only
Bacon	Nuts
Lamb	Peanuts
Poultry	Peanut butter when not hydrogenated
Sausage	Soybeans
Coconut oil	Avocados
Margarine	Fish oils
Lard	Fatty fish (tuna or mackerel)
Eggs	
Chocolate	
Peanut butter when hydrogenated	
Hydrogenated vegetable shortening	
Liverwurst and other luncheon meats	
Hot dogs	
Salad dressings such as mayonnaise, French dressings, Thousand Island, etc.	

APPENDIX 7

SUGAR

One of the main reasons that women have PMS is because of the excessive simple sugars in their diet. This occurs not only because of eating simple sugars that you know about, but also because of eating the sugars that you may not know about. Many of you may be surprised to find out how much simple sugars can be found in the foods that you eat. Yet more often than not you are unaware of. As we discussed earlier, certain foods may not at first appear to have significant amounts of simple carbohydrates within them. They may also not appear to be made up of substantial content that will upon your eating be transformed into or act exactly like simple sugars. There are many such foods, for example, white rice and processed white flour will almost instantly be transformed into simple sugars during the digestion process.

In the following table we will list the percentage of the total content of a number of foods which either are made up of substantial simple sugars or acts like simple sugars upon eating them. This list is by no means exhaustive in listing the simple sugar content of all processed and refined foods. Such a list would virtually be useless as it would go on for pages and it is likely no one would be interested. Instead, we recommend that you read product labels, looking for sugar content if it is present, and for total carbohydrate content, and always read the list of ingredients and look for names you know to be simple sugars. If you do this regularly, you will be capable of being fully in control of the amount of sugars in your diet. Remember in many foods the sugar content is hidden by calling it: dextrose, sucrose, lactose, fructose, dextro-maltin or dextro-maltose, corn sweetener, corn syrup, corn or modified food starch, molasses, maple syrup, honey, etc.

FOOD	% SUGAR
Cherry Jell-O	82.6%
Coffee-mate	65.0%
Hershey bar	51.0%
Shake 'N Bake BBQ Style	51.0%
Sara Lee Chocolate cake	40.0%
Wishbone Russian Dressing	30.0%
Ketchup	29.0%
Quaker 100% Natural cereal	24.0%
Hamburger Helper	23.0%
Cool Whip	21.0%
Ice Cream	21.0%
Libby's Peaches	18.0%

30 Days To No More PMS
The Cook Book

FOOD	% SUGAR
Bouillon cubes	14.8%
Commercial yogurt	13.7%
Ritz crackers	12.0%
Whole kernel corn (canned)	10.7%
Skippy Peanut butter	9.2%
Coke (9 tsp./12 oz.)	8.8%
Wishbone Italian Dressing	7.3%
Spaghetti sauce	6.2%

CEREALS READY TO EAT - % SUGAR:

For simplicity those products with "*sugar*" in their title have been left out.

King Vitamin	58.5%
Apple Jacks	55.0%
B ran Buds	45.7%
Alpha Bits	40.3%
Fortified Oat Flakes	22.2%
All Bran	20.0%
40% Bran Flakes (Kelloggs)	16.2%
Granola	16.0%
Granola (dates or raisins)	14.5%
Life	14.5%
Raisin Bran	10.0%
Rice Chex	8.5%
Total	8.1%
Corn Flakes	7.8%
Corn Chex	7.5%
Crisp Rice	7.3%
Wheaties	4.7%
Corn Total	4.4%
Special K	4.4%
Post Toasties	4.1%
Product 19	4.1%

30 Days To No More PMS
The Cook Book

FOOD	% SUGAR
Puffed Wheat	3.5%
Grape Nut Flakes	3.3%
Wheat Chex	2.6%
Cheerios	2.2%
Shredded Wheat	1.0%

HINTS FOR ELIMINATING SUGAR FROM YOUR DIET

Avoid or do the following:

1. Avoid dessert foods, bakery goods, cookies, ice cream, yogurt with fruit, frozen yogurt, non-diet soft drinks and candy all contain sugar or honey.

2. Avoid foods you may not recognize as having sugar: unsweetened foods, canned foods, canned or packaged vegetables and fruits, bouillon cubes, non-dairy creamers, catsup, cereals, TV dinners. Check the label, look at sugar content and ingredients.

3. Do use fresh raw fruit for your sweet tooth. Eat as fresh as possible, the way they come off the tree.

4. Avoid canned, bottled or frozen fruit juices as they usually have been cooked (concentrated and Pasturized, hence they have been processed) and often have sugar added.

5. Do not use commercially cooked fruits in place of fresh fruits as their vitamins and minerals may have been significantly destroyed and the sugars may have become similar to processed sugars.

6. Use dried fruits only as a confection - no more than once daily - watch for added sulfur and sugar in commercially prepared dried fruits.

7. Do not use artificial sweeteners. They keep you addicted to sweets, they are food additives and may be potentially dangerous chemicals.

30 Days To No More PMS
The Cook Book

8. Do learn to enjoy the natural goodness of grains, fruits and vegetables.

9. Do not use products which say they have *"Fructose"* in them. When Fructose is advertized on a label of a processed food is really sucrose, table sugar or at least it is now a simple sugar. Once fructose is cooked, it is modified and acts like sucrose.

REVIEW - ALL THESE ARE EITHER SUGAR OR ACT LIKE SUGAR:
White-table sugar, raw sugar, brown sugar, turbinado sugar, honey, maple sugar, maple syrup, molasses, corn syrup, corn sweetener, invert sugar, fructose, dextrose, maltose, malto-dextrose, sucrose, barley sweetener, corn starch, modified corn starch, modified food starch, alcohol, glucose, lactose, white flour, bleached flour, rice flour, rice vinegar, rice sweetener, processed mashed potatoes most refined foods and any ingredient which ends in -ose. These are all sugars or act like sugars and should be avoided in the week to two weeks prior to the onset of your menstrual periods.

This list was presented primarily to stimulate your interest in how much *sugar* may be found in foods you may not otherwise think have sugar at all. For further information you are advised to check your local library or health food store for books which list sugar content of specific foods. Remember read labels!

APPENDIX 8

HOW TO DECREASE CALORIES AND LOSE WEIGHT WHILE TREATING YOUR PMS

PMS women tend to be 10 -15 lbs. or more, heavier than their non-PMS women counterparts. This may be because of what PMS women eat that has caused them to have PMS in the first place. It is clearly often related to the increased appetite that is commonly seen in PMS women. The PMS promoting diet tends to be high in sweets, refined foods and simple carbohydrates, high in dairy, and filled with low quality (empty-calorie junk) foods. This type of diet is high in calorie and high in fat content and leads to weight gain. Weight gain leads to increase body fat and since estrogen is stored in fat cells, the greater the amount of body fat the higher the circulating and stored estrogen which leads to PMS.

As many PMS women see themselves as overweight, they are often likely to become depressed. They may then want sweets to appease their depression and accompanying frustration. They often experience self-directed anger. They may feel progressively more hopeless and ultimately find themselves saying or thinking, "Why should I stay on any diet, when I can't control myself and I can't seem to control my weight?" They may then starve themselves to lose weight. Without realizing it starvation further reduces their intake of essential nutrients and this only potentiate their PMS symptoms. This entire process often worsens as they become more and more nutritionally deficient.

It is most important that women who have poor self-images because of their weight or their PMS have a plan to help them lose weight while they are eliminating their PMS. It is most important that any attempt at weight loss be planned with a strong *intention to win*. That is, understanding how to lose weight and creating a program that takes into consideration her PMS and the guidelines already given to you to eliminate and prevent return of the PMS symptoms.

SOME SPECIFIC INSTRUCTIONS:

1. Read through this book to understand the basics of PMS Nutritional Treatment program.
2. DO NOT START TO SERIOUSLY DIET UNTIL YOU ARE SIGNIFICANTLY SYMPTOM FREE.
3. While starting into the PMS--Nutritional Treatment program, consider choosing foods that are lower in calories and higher in overall nutrition.
4. Read through the list of suggestions below and *use* them as often as possible.

30 Days To No More PMS
The Cook Book

SPECIFIC SUGGESTIONS TO HELP YOU LOSE WEIGHT:

1. Watch your total calorie consumption - that means that both foods and drinks count. If you are trying to create a permanently slim you, it is important to remember that the effects of calories are cumulative. Maintain necessary food consumption by choosing lower calorie foods. **Don't starve yourself**, this is neither healthy nor does starvation diets result in permanent weight loss. It can also worsen your PMS symptoms.

2. Eat at least four to six small meals a day. Skipping a meal often leads a dieter to snack heavily or eat too much at the next meal. Be patient. It may take several weeks to get used to eating breakfast. But "breaking the fast" is very important in regulating the appetite.

3. *Eat Slowly and Chew Deliberately*. If you find yourself eating too rapidly, put your fork down after each bite of food. It takes twenty minutes for the appetite center in your hypothalamus to get the message that you are ingesting food. Until it gets that message, your brain will continue to send out the hunger signals to which you are already responding. If you are eating quickly, you will likely eat much more food than you actually need to eat before your brain sends out satiation signals. To get a head start on your hypothalamus, you may wish to eat a small low-calorie portion of your meal ten minutes before you actually sit down to the main course.

4. Start your dinner with a salad, but choose a low-calorie dressing and use it sparingly. Regular calorie dressing may be used, but only in limited quantities of, at most, one to two tablespoons at most. (See Appendix 6, Low Fat Eating.)

5. Give yourself a psychological advantage by using smaller plates. This will fulfill your psychological need to see a full plate while reducing caloric intake. It really works. Try it!

6. Purposely leave small amounts of food on your plate, even if it is only a few pieces of corn. The "clean plate" syndrome has been the downfall of many well-intentioned dieters. When there is just a little bit of food left on the plate, it should become a new signal to stop eating.

7. Cut down on fats and oils. Fat and oils are the most concentrated sources of calories--two and a quarter times more concentrated than carbohydrates (grains and vegetables). Trim most visible fat from all meats before you cook them. Cut off or drain all the remaining fat before

30 Days To No More PMS
The Cook Book

you serve your food. Broil or BBQ so fat can drip off and away from your eating it. Pick leaner cuts of meat, if you do not know which they are ask your butcher, they are usually the cheaper cuts.

8. Eat smaller portions of meat. Per serving, meat contains more calories than any other food group, and most Americans consume far more meat than they actually need. Limit yourself to one or two 4 (but no greater than 6) oz. servings daily.

9. Whole grain bread provides significant nutrition (white and bleached flour breads are empty-calorie substances), but be careful of what you spread on it! Jelly (50 calories per tbsp.), apple butter (32 calories), margarine (100 calories) and butter (100 calories). While all will provide a few nutrients, they are in the end a poor choice for the women who want to rid themselves of her PMS. Peanut butter (81 calories) does contain significant nutrients and is high in magnesium. Use this when you need a midday snack.

10. Be careful how you prepare potatoes. Minimize your consumption of fat and stay away from: fried potatoes, hash browns, home fries, french fries, potato sticks and potato chips. You can, if you desire, fry foods in a Teflon pan either without oil or using only a very small amount of oil. You can if you wish stir fry foods using water or defatted chicken, beef or vegetable broth only. Cut down on your normal amount of butter and sour cream on baked potatoes.

11. Increase the amount of vegetables in your diet, especially the low-calorie, non-starchy ones. Besides providing bulk, color and essential vitamins, they usually require you to chew deliberately, thereby giving the food message time to reach your hypothalamus.

12. Watch leftovers! Beware of the "I'll-Just-Finish-This-Up" attitude. You may not want the leftover food to go to waste, but if you eat it, it will go to *your waist*. Have someone else clean up after every meal. Dispose of scraps by putting them directly into your garbage disposal unit, garbage can, or wrap leftovers immediately and refrigerate or freeze them.

13. When possible, buy food in exactly the quantity you plan to eat. That extra ounce you get for practically nothing for buying the larger size will probably show up around your waist. Ultimately, you must decide if that risk is outweighed by the price "savings" for purchasing in bulk

14. Break the habit of treating or rewarding yourself with food. Reward yourself by feeling

30 Days To No More PMS
The Cook Book

good about the calories you have saved. Buy a new dress, go to the gym, get a massage, have your nails, hair or toe nails done to reward yourself, don't use food.

15. Weigh yourself as little as possible and certainly, if you must, no more than once a week. *If you must weigh yourself: 1)* Reconsider this choice, for as we suggested earlier this is not a good idea for you will tend to be unhappy, if your weight loss does not meet your current expectations. If you must weigh your self then always do it at the same time, on the same scale, under the same conditions. Rather than weighing yourself, if you must monitor your progress, do it by dress size or waist, thigh or breast measurements and watch those numbers decrease.

16. Be aware of the cues that trigger your appetite. If seeing food is the cue that sets you off, then keep food out of sight as much as possible.

17. Wrap and seal things tightly and elaborately. Tape shut the lids of jars and tins. This maneuver will cut down on aromatic (smell) cues. Also, you may decide that this is just too much bother to unwrap and rewrap the container for a little nibble.

18. If you are still eating a lot of processed and refined foods, read the labels to see exactly how much fat is in the foods you are eating. Note at the top of the Nutritional Facts Label that comes with each product, how many fat calories are in the food you are about to buy.

It is hoped that these suggestions will be of value to you in controlling what you eat on a daily basis and how many you should allow in order to support your weight loss. It is also important to have an idea of just how many calories are allowed to you to either maintain your weight or to lose weight.

FURTHER IDEAS FOR WEIGHT LOSS:

1. Think of losing in *ounces* and not in pounds. There are 16 ounces in a pound. Each pound represents some 3,500 stored calories. Each ounce represents 220 calories. It is much easier to eliminate 220 calories worth of calories, then to try to lose pounds of calories. If you decrease your calorie intake by 440 calories a day, in one week you will lose 2 ounces a day or 14 ounces a week or 4 pounds per month. This is a safe and reliable amount of weight to lose, it means that you have cut down extra calories and that you are still eating and not

30 Days To No More PMS
The Cook Book

starving.

2. Increase your physical activity. The more calories you burn the less food you will have to give up or the faster you will lose weight. Walking one of the very best and safest exercises. Walk 15 to 20 minutes a day each day or 30 minutes a day three to four times a week. See our section on Exercise in our book, *30 Days To No More PMS, A Doctor's Proven Nutritional Program* for specific details and suggestions.

3. Pick a realistic goal based not on fantasy, but on reality, what you can actually do or obtain. Create several mini-goals. Instead of wanting to lose 10 lbs. in one month, work toward losing 1 to 2 lbs. per week which will ultimately, net you 15 to 20 lbs. of weight loss two to three months and 30 to 40 lbs.

4. Don't try to lose weight too fast, be realistic, a good goal *that works* is generally one pound per week for each week you are trying.

HOW YOU CAN CREATE YOUR WEIGHT LOSS SAFELY

1. Multiply your present weight by 15 to get the number of calories you need daily to maintain your present weight.

2. Subtract 500 calories from this figure. This will give you a deficit of 3,500 calories a week which will enable you to lose about a pound a week. The final calorie amount you end up with will be your daily calorie budget while reducing.

3. If you can use calorie tables, if easily available you, to calculate the total calories of all the various foods you chose to eat. Remember to stay within the PMS dietary plan.

APPENDIX 9

THE B VITAMINS

Even though we tend to talk about individual vitamins, one at a time, it is important to understand that vitamins do not act singly. They require other vitamins and minerals along with proteins to make enzymes and coenzyme which are essential for your body to run optimally. These interactions with other nutrient are important and ultimately affect every cell in your body.

Enzymes and coenzyme are necessary as they act as facilitators in the metabolic processes of the body. The B vitamins are of importance in maintaining and sustaining those processes involved in converting food into energy. The B vitamins are intimately involved in the metabolism of sugar. The B vitamins are needed as the sugar reaches the cells and after it is used by them, to remove waste products.

A deficiency in only one of the B vitamins is unlikely, as you read along please notice the sources of all of the B vitamins are basically very similar. A diet that is low in one of any of the B vitamins will most likely also be low in several others or all of them.

VITAMIN B1 (THIAMINE)

The disease created when one suffers from a deficiency of vitamin B1 is called *Beriberi*. Over the years millions of men, women and children have died of this disease. One of nature's best sources of vitamin B's is whole grain rice, when men began milling rice to produce white rice, the death toll in the Orient from beriberi rose into the millions, and possibly even into hundreds of millions.

Beriberi is a disease is caused through the following steps and stages; starches and sugars are ingested, they are converted into energy for the body cells, pyruvic acid is manufactured during this process. As pyruvic acid accumulates as a waste product, vitamin B1 is required to eliminate this excess of pyruvic acid. If there is insufficient vitamin B1 the blood levels of pyruvic acid rise and when it becomes too high the illness that is caused is beriberi.

In human beings a deficiency of vitamin B1 will often lead to some of the following symptoms: decreased basal metabolism, decreased ability to function and work, forgetfulness, irritability, quarrelsomeness, increased appetite, apathy, confusion, fatigue, numbness of hands and feet, nausea and vomiting, agitation and depression. These symptoms are listed to give you an appreciation of the kinds of symptoms that can occur when a vitamin deficiency state exists. For interest sake, compare the symptoms we have just given to you as signs of a vitamin B1 deficiency with the symptoms attributed to PMS. Notice the similarities of many of the symptoms.

Vitamin B1 is also found in organ meats such as kidney, heart, liver, whole wheat, wheat germ, yeast, rice bran and rice polish, brown rice, peanuts, peas, pecans, walnuts, lima beans, lean pork and soybeans and soy flour.

Vitamin B1 like all other B vitamins can be destroyed by heat, especially boiling. However, they are not destroyed by steaming. The B vitamins are diminished in the body by fever, surgical operations and other stresses.

VITAMIN B2 (RIBOFLAVIN)

Some of the symptoms which occur when there is a shortage of vitamin B2 are: sore, dry chapped lips, painful cracks in the corner of the lips which may not heal readily. A long-standing deficiency of vitamin B2 may cause little wrinkles radiating from the mouth. Deficiency of Vitamin B2 may lead to decreased tears and increased small blood vessels in the whites of the eyes. One also might have increased discomfort with glare and bright sun light. Deficiency of vitamin B2 may affect the body's ability to ward off disease and infection. Deficiency may lead to severe breaking out on the scrotum or around the vagina. The tongue may develop soreness and burning as well as loss of the sensation of taste.

Vitamin B2 thought to be one of the most common vitamin deficiencies in the United States. Vitamin B2 is found in liver, kidneys, wheat germ, peanuts, turnup greens, mushrooms, peas, collard greens, kale, soy beans and soy four, yeast, eggs, milk and milk products. These are the richest sources of this vitamin. It can easily be destroyed by heat. How much of these foods do you eat fresh, uncooked or unprocessed?

VITAMIN B3 (NIACIN)

Niacin is a B vitamin that is involved primarily in releasing energy from the foods we eat. Deficiency of niacin reduces our ability to utilize food. Without niacin the body runs inefficiently, food is inappropriately metabolized and this leads to many different types of physical disturbances and symptoms. Niacin deficiency in its extreme is called *Pellagra*. It is known by its "four D's," dermatitis, dementia, diarrhea and death. In its mildest form, niacin deficiency may cause symptoms such as dizziness, neuritis (pain, numbness or tingling), baldness, insomnia, arthritis, acne, indigestion, bad breath, phlebitis (inflammation of a vein), constipation, headache, conjunctivitis (inflammation of the outer layer of the eye), muscular weakness, fatigue, and even tender gums. It has also been incriminated as a factor in atherosclerosis (hardening of the arteries) and high blood pressure. It is involved with hydrochloric acid (stomach-digestive acid) production in the stomach, there by affecting digestion and the absorption of other necessary nutrients. It is less heat, light, acid and alkali affected, therefore more efficient than most of the other B vitamins. It is available in three forms, niacinamide, nicotinic acid, and nicotinamide these are synthetic forms as versed to niacin itself.

Niacin is used as a coenzyme and assists enzymes in the metabolism (break down) of proteins, fats and carbohydrates. Here again, as a B vitamin it is involved with sugar metabolism. The exact role of niacin in PMS is unknown but its effect on improving circulation and reducing blood cholesterol is of vital importance to the PMS woman.

Niacin is found in rice bran, rice polishings, roasted peanuts, liver, yeast, mushrooms, almonds, wheat, turkey, veal, chicken and peas.

PANTOTHENIC ACID

Pantothenic acid was discovered by the famed Biochemist, Roger Williams. He described it as extremely important in protecting against stress. It acts as part of Coenzyme A and functions in the creation and breakdown of many vital compounds involved in body chemistry. It is essential in the intermediary metabolism of carbohydrates, fats, and proteins. It is generally found in many green vegetables and organ meats such as liver and kidney. It is also found in eggs, salmon, and yeast, wheat germ, rice bran and rice polish.

Symptoms of Pantothenic acid deficiency include neuritis and neuralgia affecting the nervous system and causing burning, tingling and numbness in the arms, hands, legs and feet. Also weakness, fatigue, a decrease in spontaneous activity, changes in mood, dizziness, unsteadiness in walking, cramps, lethargy, and even psychosis, have all been attributed to a deficiency of Pantothenic acid.

30 Days To No More PMS
The Cook Book

VITAMIN B 12 (Cyanocobalamin)

Vitamin B12 is most important for the prevention of *Pernicious Anemia* (PA). PA was first isolated in 1948 although the treatment of Pernicious anemia with B12 was first established in 1926 when Minot and Murphy suggested to their patients to eat liver as a treatment of their PA symptoms. It is now known that as little as one-millionth of a gram of vitamin B12 injected per day (a gram is one-twenty-eighth of an ounce) can prevent Pernicious anemia. Vitamin B12 is made in our body by bacteria in our intestinal tract. The nerve cells of the central nervous system seem to be dependent on it. Unlike the other B vitamins, B12 can be stored in our liver. A vitamin B12 rich diet can allow as much as three years supply to be stockpiled within the liver. Pregnancy increases the need for this vitamin.

B12 is involved with the metabolism of single-carbon fragments, it is essential for the production of nucleic acids and nucleoprotein (our RNA and DNA- genetic materials), and is extremely important for the formation of normal red blood cells. It also has a significant role in the metabolism of nervous tissues and plays a role in the breakdown of fats into energy for our body.

Symptoms of PA are generally related to the gastrointestinal tract and include loss of appetite, constipation, diarrhea, vague abdominal pain. Burning of the tongue is often one of the earliest symptom, and loss of weight and fever are usual.

Liver and kidney are the best sources of vitamin B12. Vegetarian diets are usually lacking in adequate vitamin B12 as there are only insignificant traces found in fruits, vegetables, and grains. Meats and eggs, as well as milk and dairy foods, contain limited amounts of vitamin B12.

BIOTIN

A deficiency of biotin can cause changes in the skin and the tongue, loss of appetite, heart symptoms, sluggishness, as well as intense depression occasionally with hallucinations. Use of raw eggs in the diet can promote biotin deficiency.

Its action in the body is still poorly understood, but it is believed to be an essential component of a coenzyme. It appears to be involved in the production and breakdown of fatty acids (precursors of fat) and amino acids (the building blocks of proteins). It can be produced in our own intestinal tract.

30 Days To No More PMS
The Cook Book

Sources of biotin are liver, mushrooms, brown rice, soybeans and soy flour, peanuts, yeast, milk, meats, egg yolks, most vegetables, bananas, grapefruit, tomatoes, watermelon, and strawberries.

FOLIC ACID

Folic acid deficiency causes anemia. Folic acid appears to be essential for production of nucleic acids (once again RNA and DNA) and normal fat breakdown and metabolism as well as in the final maturing of red blood cells. It can be produced within our own intestinal tract.

Folic acid is found in dark green leafy vegetables, organ meats, liver, beef, wheat, eggs, fish, dry beans, lentils, lima beans, wheat germ, roasted peanuts, asparagus, potatoes and cowpeas.

OTHER B VITAMINS

Inositol, choline, and para-aminobenzoic acid are also B vitamins about which too little is known in relations to PMS. They are supplied by the same foods that are the best sources of the other B vitamins.

All of the B vitamins are interrelated with the role of magnesium in our body.

APPENDIX 10

VITAMIN B6

It should be clear by now that vitamin B6 plays an essential role in the creation and treatment of PMS. We have presented a good deal of evidence in earlier sections. Now you will need to concentrate on obtaining adequate levels of vitamin B6 from your diet. The problem is that vitamin B6 is most commonly found in foods that are also high in calcium. In this appendix we are providing you with a list of foods which are not only high in vitamin B6, but also high in magnesium.

FOOD	SERVING SIZE	AMOUNT OF B6
Rice bran	¼ cup	.8*
Rice polishings	¼ cup	.8
Soybeans	½ cup	.8
Banana	1 medium	.6
Buckwheat flour	1 cup	.6
Navy beans	½ cup	.6
Lentils	½ cup	.6
Lima beans	½ cup	.5
Pinto	½ cup	.5
Black-eyed	½ cup	.48
Avocado	½ medium	.46
Whole Wheat flour	1 cup	.4
Potato	1 cup diced	.38
Rye flour	1 cup	.38
Brown rice	⅓ cup	.34
Wheat germ	¼ cup	.3
Torula yeast	1 tbsp.	.24
Lima beans, green frozen.	1 cup	.24
Green Peas	1 cup	.23
Sweet potato	1 small	.22

*Values are milligrams per 100 grams of Vitamin B6.

First notice that many of these foods are also high magnesium foods. This should make obtaining adequate Vitamin B6 and magnesium much easier. This list is by no means exhaustive. It attempts

30 Days To No More PMS
The Cook Book

to stimulate your interest in which foods are highest in Vitamin B6. If you have specific needs or interest we recommend that you check your local library or health food store for books which list Vitamin B6 content of specific foods.

APPENDIX 11

FIBER

Although dietary *fiber* is not an issue specifically related to PMS, the body's need for a proper amount of fiber is important when planning a good health diet. In recent years fiber has been recognized as an important factor in good health and well-being. Its relationship to preventing hypertension, bowel cancer, and other bowel disorders is becoming well established. In planning your meals consider making sure that you have as much fiber as you can get into it and make sure you add fiber as often as you can. In the following table we will list those foods which are high both in fiber and magnesium, while still relatively low in calcium.

FOOD — **PERCENT FIBER** *Values are listed as % volume.

Food	Percent Fiber
Wheat bran	44.0%*
All Bran, cereal	26.7%
Puffed wheat, cereal	15.4%
Soya flour	14.3%
Almonds	14.3%
Coconut, fresh	13.6%
Shredded Wheat, cereal	12.3%
Peas, frozen	12.0%
Cornflakes	11.0%
Wholemeal flour	9.6%
Wholemeal breads	8.5%
Peanuts	8.1%
Grapenuts, cereal	7.0%
Sweet corn, canned	5.7%
Special K, cereal	5.5%
Rice, brown unpolished	5.5%
Peas, fresh	5.2%
Brown bread	5.1%
Corn on the cob, boiled	4.7%
Rice Krispies, cereal	4.5%
Lentils, split	3.7%
Bananas	3.4%
Potatoes, baked	2.5%

If you have a fiber problem this list will help you to become as selective as possible.

APPENDIX 12

HOW TO ELIMINATE SALT FROM YOUR DIET

In order to avoid foods high in salt content you have to 1) decrease eating foods high in salt content 2) not add extra salt 3) know which foods are high in salt content. In this section we will give you valuable hints to reduce salt and provide you with a list of foods with their salt content so that you can better control the amount of salt in your diet. This list is NOT extensive but rather contains the more common foods. If you have further needs about specific foods, you will have to search out the answers yourself.

HINTS:
1. Avoid processed foods and delicatessen type foods and pickled foods.
2. Avoid canned foods...soups, tomato juice, vegetables.
3. Avoid prepared and frozen foods.
4. Avoid salty snacks...pretzels, crackers, popcorn, nuts and chips.
5. Avoid prepared meats...bacon, ham, sausages, cold cuts.
6. Avoid processed cheeses and cheese spreads, and most cheeses.
7. Avoid salty or smoked fish...canned tuna, sardines, anchovies, caviar, herring, salted or dried cod, smoked salmon.
8. Avoid prepared mustards, horseradish, catsup.
9. Avoid soy sauce, bullion cubes, seasoning mixes, dried soups, soups which contain monosodium glutamate.
10. When dining out ask that no salt or monosodium glutamate be added to your food.
11. Eliminate or cut down on salt in cooking at home.
12. Use herbs or spices, lemon juice, garlic or onions instead for flavoring your foods.
13. Try not to salt foods at the table and if necessary only to taste.

SALT CONTENT OF SELECTED FOODS

FOOD	SERVING SIZE	MG SALT
Ham, cured	3 oz.	675 mg.
Frankfurter	1	540 mg.
Bologna	1 slice	390 mg.
Beef, veal	3 oz.	75 mg.
Lamb, pork	3 oz.	75 mg.
Bacon	1 slice	75 mg.

30 Days To No More PMS
The Cook Book

FOOD	SERVING SIZE	MG SALT
Chicken	3 oz.	75 mg.
Fish, fresh	3 oz.	75 mg.
Egg	1 whole	60 mg.

BEANS AND NUTS:

Peanuts, salted	¼ cup	275 mg.
Dry beans, peas	½ cup	15 mg.
Peanuts, unsalted	¼ cup	2 mg.

VEGETABLES AND FRUITS:

Carrots, celery, spinach	½ cup	40 mg.
Cabbage, lettuce, radishes, turnip	½ cup	15 mg.
Corn, cucumbers, green peppers, lima beans, onions, peas, potatoes, pumpkin, sweet potato, tomato, egg plant	1 cup	5 mg.
Most fruits	½ cup	2 mg.

BREADS AND CEREALS

Oatmeal, cooked and salted	1 cup	520 mg.
Bran flakes	3/4 cup	340 mg.
Whole wheat bread	1 slice	170 mg.
Corn flakes	1 cup	165 mg.
Wheat germ	¼ cup	5 mg.
Rice, cooked	½ cup	3 mg.
Puffed wheat, puffed rice, shredded wheat	1 cup	1 mg.

MILK, CHEESE AND DAIRY PRODUCTS:

Buttermilk	1 cup	225 mg.
Cheese-cheddar, Swiss, American	1 oz.	220 mg.
Low fat cheese	1 oz.	200 mg.
Cottage cheese, creamed	¼ cup	160 mg.
Low fat milk	1 cup	120 mg.
Cottage cheese, unsalted	¼ cup	30 mg.

30 Days To No More PMS
The Cook Book

Food	Serving Size	Mg Salt
Parmesan cheese	1 tbsp.	40 mg.

FOOD	SERVING SIZE	MG SALT
MISCELLANEOUS FOODS:		
Dill pickle	1 large	1,928 mg.
Soy sauce	1 tbsp.	1,300 mg.
Salt	¼ tsp.	575 mg.
Miso	1 tbsp.	500 mg.
Homemade soup, salt	1 cup	500 mg.
Gelatin, flavored (4-5 servings)	1 box	330 mg.
Worcestershire sauce	1 tbsp.	315 mg.
Catsup	1 tbsp.	200 mg.
Potato chips	10	200 mg.
Salad dressing	1 tbsp.	200 mg.
Green olive	1	155 mg.
Margarine, salted	1 tbsp.	110 mg.
Peanut butter, regular	1 tbsp.	18 mg.
Gelatin, plain	1 tbsp.	3 mg.
Margarine, unsalted	1 tbsp.	1 mg.

FOODS LOW IN SALT:

1. Whole grains and legumes prepared without salt.
2. Most fruits and vegetables.
3. These are the foods basic to the PMS woman's diet.

APPENDIX 13

ABBREVIATIONS

WEIGHTS AND MEASUREMENTS

tsp. = teaspoon	5 milliliters	3 tsp	= 1 tbsp.
tbsp. = tablespoon	15 milliliters	4 tbsp	= ¼ cup
c. = cup	8 fluid oz	240 milliliters	
	1 cup	= 16 tbsp	
	1 cup	= ½ pint	
pt. = pint	1 pint	= 2 cups	
qt. = quart	= 1 quart	4 cups	= about 1 liter
	4 quarts	= 1 gallon	
lt. = liter	= 1000 ml		
ml. = milliliter	= 1 cc		
	1.25 ml.	= ¼ tsp	
lb. = pounds	= 1 lb.	454 grams	
gm. = gram	28 gm	= 1 oz.	
oz. =ounce	= 1 oz	3.5 oz.	= 100 grams
Slow oven	= 300-325 degrees F.		
Moderate oven	= 350-375 degrees F.		
Hot oven	= 400-425 degrees F.		
Very hot oven	= 450 degrees F.		

GOOD EATING!

AND

GOODBYE PMS!

30 Days To No More PMS
The Cook Book

PMS FORMS FOR PERSONAL USE

> ### Please Note:
>
> All of the forms found in this section
> and more, can be found at
> www.30DaysToNoMorePMS.com
> in the PMS Forms Section.

You may give any of our PMS Forms, free of charge,
to any person, man or woman,
who you believe may need or be interested in them.

30 Days To No More PMS
The Cook Book

10 Most Frequent Foods You Eat

1. _____
2. _____
3. _____
4. _____
5. _____
6. _____
7. _____
8. _____
9. _____
10. _____

Comments:

30 Days To No More PMS
The Cook Book

The PMS Evaluation Questionnaire (PEQ) Self Evaluation Test

The PEQ Test offered below can help you to determine whether or not you have PMS and how sever your PMS actually is. To determine for yourself please complete the PEQ Self Evaluation Test below.

1. Using the following self-grading system, we ask you to estimate the intensity of your own symptoms between 0 and 4.

2. Zero (0) would indicate that you have had no occurrences any specific PMS symptom or symptoms during the week to two weeks prior to the onset of your menstrual period.

3. A One (1) would indicate that at some time during the period of one to two weeks prior to the onset of your menstrual period, you are having minimal PMS symptoms.

4. A Two (2) would indicate that at some time during the period of one to two weeks prior to the onset of your menstrual period, you are having mild to moderate PMS symptoms.

5. A Three (3) would indicate that at some time during the period of one to two weeks prior to the onset of your menstrual period, you are having moderate to severe PMS symptoms.

6. A Four (4) would indicate that at some time during the period of two weeks prior to the onset of your menstrual period, you are partially or completely disabled because of one or more PMS symptoms.

7. This means that listing a score of 1, 2, 3 or 4 requires that you judge that you are having PMS symptoms and that they are mild, moderate, severe or disabling in their intensity.

8. After you have completely filled numbers in each and every box as instructed above and below that you will then total each of the columns.

9. Be sure to enter your name, the date and the first day of your last menstrual period above.

10. Once you have totaled your scores, subtract the total of the far right column from the far left column:

    If the difference is below 12, you most likely do not have PMS. Of your score is grater than 12 but below 18 this represents borderline to mild PMS. From 19 to 25 represents mild to moderate PMS. From 25 to 35 represents moderate to severe PMS. From 35 to 45 represents severe PMS. 45 or greater represents disabling PMS.

30 Days To No More PMS
The Cook Book

PMS Evaluation Questionnaire (PEQ)

Your Name _____ Date _____ Last Menstrual Period ___/___/___

Grade Your Symptoms For Your Menstrual Cycle

	A Week Before Period	B Week During Period	C Week After Period	
Symptoms				**Total from Week Before Scores (Column A)**
Nervous Tension				
Mood Swings				
Irritability				
Anxiety				
	Total	Total	Total	
Weight Gain				**Subtract (—) Total from Week After Scores (Column C)**
Swelling of Breast				
Abdominal				
	Total	Total	Total	
Headache				**Equals (=)**
Craving for Sweets				
Increased Appetite				
Heart Pounding				
Fatigue				
Dizziness or				
	Total	Total	Total	**The Severity of Your PMS Symptoms**
Depression				
Forgetfulness				
Crying				
Confusion				
Insomnia				
Add Your Score	Total Column A	Total Col B	Total Col C	

Personal Management Diary - Daily Symptoms Record

Name: _____ Date: ____/____/_____

Grading of Menses (Menstrual Flow)	0-none	3-heavy
	1-slight	4-heavy and clots
	2-moderate	

Grading of Symptoms (Complaints)	0-none	3-severe
	1-mild	4-disabling
	2-moderate	

Day of	1	2	3	4	5	6	7	8	9	10	11	12	13	14	15	16	17	18	19	20	21	22	23	24	25	26	27	28	29	30	31	32	33	34	35
Date																																			
Menstrual Flow																																			

PMS-A Anxiety Group

Nervous Tension																																			
Mood																																			
Irritability																																			
Anxiety																																			

PMS-C Cravings Group

Headache																																			
Craving for Sweets																																			
Increased Appetite																																			
Heart Pounding																																			
Fatigue																																			
Dizziness/ Faintness																																			

PMS-D Depression Group

Depression																																			
Forgetfulness																																			
Crying																																			
Confusion																																			
Insomnia																																			

PMS-H Hydrous Group

Weight Gain																																			
Swelling Extremities																																			
Breast Tenderness																																			
Abdominal Bloating																																			

Dysmenorrhea - Painful Menstruation

Cramps, Abdominal Pain																																			
Backache																																			
General																																			

Other Symptoms

Weight

Weight in lbs.																																			

Vitamins-Medications

Vitamins																																			
Medication																																			

One Week Sample Menu

	Sunday	Monday	Tuesday	Wednesday	Thursday	Friday	Saturday
Breakfast							
AM Snack							
Lunch							
Afternoon Snack							
Dinner							
PM Snack							

30 Days To No More PMS
The Cook Book

Comments-Thoughts- Notes:

30 Days To No More PMS
The Cook Book

Foot Notes:

1. In this book PMS, PMTS and PMT are for our purposes, all treated with the same dietary program.

2. For clarity sake, we differentiate between the concepts of treatment and cure. Cure represents a situation where you find a permanent solution to a problem, while treatment suggests that there either will be resolution over time helped or caused by the treatment program, or that there is no solution, but rather an on-going temporary approach to the situation. In PMS, "cure" represents a diet which maintains proper levels of necessary nutrients thereby establishing a permanent solution.

3. A unit can be defined as a specific quantity of food, for example: milligrams, gram, ounce, teaspoon, tablespoon, 100 grams, etc. For our purposes it would represent milligrams. The purpose of using it this way is to be able to compare amounts of magnesium and calcium found in foods rather than amounts of the specific foods themselves. See Appendices 2 and 3 for more detailed discussion.

4. Women: 15 to 18 years old, 400 IU vitamin D; 19-22 years old, 300 IU vitamin D; 23-50 years of age, 200 IU vitamin D daily.

5. RDA is 800 milligrams per day.

6. Remember, if you overeat you will most likely gain weight. The emphasis is on *small planned meals* and *not simply eating everything in sight.*

7. The values for these lists were taken from multiple sources. These lists represent only a limited number of foods available at your market and do not represent restaurant foods at all. They are to be simply used as a guide.

Printed in Great Britain
by Amazon